# BIG IDEAS

# Also by Don Tapscott

*The Blockchain Revolution: How the Technology Behind Bitcoin Is Changing Money, Business, and the World*, Penguin Portfolio, 2018
Co-author, Alex Tapscott

*Blockchain Revolution for the Enterprise Specialization*
INSEAD and Coursera, 2019
Co-instructor, Alex Tapscott

*The Digital Economy: Rethinking Promise and Peril in the Age of Networked Intelligence*, McGraw-Hill, Anniversary Edition, 2014

*Macrowikinomics: Rebooting Business and the World,*
Penguin Portfolio, 2010
Co-author, Anthony D. Williams

*Grown Up Digital: How the Net Generation Is Changing Your World,*
McGraw-Hill, 2008

*Wikinomics: How Mass Collaboration Changes Everything,*
Penguin Portfolio, 2006
Co-author, Anthony D. Williams

*The Naked Corporation: How the Age of Transparency Will Revolutionize Business,* Free Press, 2003
Co-author, David Ticoll

*Digital Capital: Harnessing the Power of Business Webs,*
Harvard Business Press, 2000
Co-authors, David Ticoll and Alex Lowy

*Blueprint to the Digital Economy: Creating Wealth in
the Era of E-Business,* McGraw-Hill, 1999
Co-authors, David Ticoll and Alex Lowy

*Growing Up Digital: The Rise of the Net Generation,*
McGraw-Hill, 1999

*The Digital Economy: Promise and Peril in the
Age of Networked Intelligence,* McGraw-Hill, 1997

*Who Knows: Safeguarding Your Privacy in a Networked World,*
McGraw-Hill, 1997
Co-author, Ann Cavoukian

*Paradigm Shift: The New Promise of Information Technology,*
McGraw-Hill Companies, 1992
Co-author, Art Caston

*Office Automation: A User-Driven Method,*
Springer, 1985

*Planning for Integrated Office Systems: A Strategic Approach,*
Carswell Legal, 1984
Co-authors, Del Henderson and Morley Greenberg

# BIG IDEAS

## Chancellor Don Tapscott
### Speaks to a New Generation
#### 2013–2019

Dr. Don Tapscott '66
CM, BA, BSc, MEd, LLD
Eleventh Chancellor (2013–2019)
of Trent University

Introduction by
Leo Groarke, President of Trent University

**BARLOW
BOOKS**

*The author acknowledges the profound generosity and scrupulous work of the Office of the Vice-President External Relations and Development at Trent University in the creation of this book.*

Library and Archives Canada Cataloguing in Publication data available upon request.

978-1-988025-72-8 (hardcover)

Printed in Canada

Publisher: Sarah Scott
Book producer: Tracy Bordian/At Large Editorial Services
Cover design: Ruth Dwight
Interior design and layout: Ruth Dwight
Copy editing: Wendy Thomas
Proofreading: Marilyn Dean

For more information, visit **www.barlowbooks.com**

Barlow Book Publishing Inc.
96 Elm Avenue, Toronto, ON
M4W 1P2 Canada

**BARLOW BOOKS**

*For the students, graduates, faculty, and
staff of Trent University who, over my seven-year term
as chancellor, gave me hope for the future of our
troubled and vulnerable planet*

# Contents

## SELECTED ARTICLES ABOUT ISSUES FACING STUDENTS

# PREFACE

## BY DON TAPSCOTT

As I write these words, Canadians are reading sickening new revelations about the consequences of the Residential Schools program in Canada. Hundreds of unmarked graves of children are being discovered weekly, victims of disease, neglect, suicide, and abuse. Their kidnapping and incarceration, predating Canadian Confederation. was part of a broader strategy of cultural genocide.

My hope is that these revelations have brought us to a turning point in Canadian history, where we will commit across the country to find justice and solutions to right the wrongs of the past and those that endure today.

Reflecting on my period as a student, volunteer, and then chancellor of Trent University, I am struck by Trent's leadership on this critical issue. At the university, there is a widespread awareness of the injustices perpetrated throughout Canada's history toward the Indigenous Peoples of Canada—and widespread anger toward those injustices. Simultaneously, there is a deep and loving respect for Indigenous culture and knowledge. This combined fight for Indigenous justice, along with commitments to making space for Indigenous voices and values and to advancing knowledge about Indigenous matters, permeates the campus.

Trent been a leader in Indigenous education for more than 50 years, when I was an undergraduate student. Led by Trent's Founding

President Thomas Symons and my fellow student (now Trent alumnus) Harvey McCue—an Anishinabe from Georgina Island First Nation—Trent became the first university in Canada (and only the second in North America) to establish an academic department dedicated to the study of Indigenous Peoples and knowledges. Today, in the Chanie Wenjack School for Indigenous Studies, Trent continues to incorporate the teachings and perspectives of elders and traditional knowledge leaders into its academic and extracurricular programming. The institution has had acclaimed Indigenous leaders Mary Simon (Canada's new Governor General) and Tom Jackson as past chancellors, predating my term. Recently, Trent added a requirement that all students, regardless of their program of study, complete one course with Indigenous content to ensure a foundational understanding of the history, traditions, cultures, and knowledge of Indigenous peoples.

This commitment goes beyond the classroom. The First Peoples House of Learning provides cultural services and academic support to diverse Indigenous learners, and offers spaces for non-Indigenous students, to build awareness and become immersed in new and traditional cultural experiences. Nozhem, Trent's 100-seat Indigenous performance theatre hosts world-class Indigenous artists and brings Indigenous youth from local First Nations to learn about and celebrate their culture through performance. Trent has a strong reciprocal relationship with the local Michi Saagiig First Nations and engages with their leadership and the Elders and Traditional Knowledge Keepers Council on such matters as land-use planning, environmental stewardship, and cultural programming. For the past 45 years, Trent has held an annual Elders and Traditional Peoples Gathering, where students and community members can listen and learn from the stories and experiences of Elders and Indigenous knowledge keepers from across the country.

As chancellor, I had the privilege of experiencing all this at Trent's remarkable convocations. Parents and supporters gather outdoors on the Bata Library podium overlooking the Otonabee (Odoonabii-ziibi) River. The academic procession is led across campus by Indigenous leaders, and members of neighboring First Nations carry their community's Eagle Staff—a sacred symbol of distinction, representing Indigenous culture and principles. A member of the Trent Aboriginal Education Council bears the Condolence Cane, a Haudenosaunee symbol representing the governing power of the Senate, the interdependent nature of the university community, and the search for knowledge in the interests of justice, equality, and peace. As remarks begin, the university's president opens with a land acknowledgement to pay tribute and respect to the First Nations people of the area, and to thank them for their ongoing care of and teachings about the land.

After all degrees are presented, graduates stand to hear the Honour Song performed by the Unity Singers—sung in Anishinaabe vocals with harmonic melodies over rhythmic drumming. During dozens of convocations, I'm pretty sure that each had a different Honour Song performed. Altogether, it makes for an unforgettable and distinctly Trent experience for all involved. There wasn't a ceremony where I left with dry eyes.

I'm pleased that Trent University has produced this tome of my speeches, writings delivered to students during my terms as chancellor. In Canada, the university chancellor has many functions, but I found the role served up a feast of opportunities to learn from the community and to share my thoughts on pertinent topics. I'm surprised that my musings during that period ended up being book size.

Many universities today are still places of critical thinking and not just vocational training.

But there is something about Trent that cultivates big ideas and motivates big action. Perhaps the idyllic campus and spectacular architecture caressing the beautiful river welcome this reflection. Perhaps Trent's founder Tom Symons, one of Canada's great public intellectuals, inbued his curiosity, his passion for ideas and truth, and his penchant for small group discussion into the university's DNA.

I witnessed this in the early years, attending Trent as an undergraduate, a mere two years after Professor Symons became the first President. I found Trent to be a place of debate, discussion, and openness to new ideas. (I remember my Biology 101 seminar that had one student in it—a big motivator for me to prepare for class discussion.) The culture was not of pure naval gazing, but of purposeful dialogue with the goal of improving the state of the world. The university has grown since then, but the culture is intact.

That's probably why Trent became a leader in exploring critical issues facing the country—most notable in my mind the horrific history and reality facing Indigenous Peoples today. Trent also had one the first environmental studies program in Canada and was the first university to achieve accreditation from ECO Canada. Trent was and is a champion of a liberal arts and sciences education.

I hope you find this book helpful regardless of whatever stage of life you find yourself in. During my period as chancellor, I addressed this and a wide range of topics about the challenges and opportunities facing young people and the broader urgent requirements of the digital age and our shrinking world. I hope these writings help you live a principled life of consequence.

*Don Tapscott*
*1 August 2021*

# AN INTRODUCTION

## BY LEO GROARKE,
## PRESIDENT OF TRENT UNIVERSITY

*It's with great pleasure that I write this introduction to a compilation of speeches and articles by Don Tapscott given to the Trent University community and related audiences during his two terms as our chancellor. I hope you will find them interesting, informative, and thoroughly enjoyable, as I did.*

Don is a great Canadian and an international authority on the impact of technology on business and society. His 1992 bestseller, *Paradigm Shift*, established him as an important thinker and commentator on these topics. *The Digital Economy*, written in 1995, introduced businesses to the transformational nature of the Internet. Two years later he helped popularize the terms "Net Generation" and the "Digital Divide" in *Growing Up Digital*. He has authored or co-authored 17 books, including *Wikinomics: How Mass Collaboration Changes Everything*, which has been translated into more than 25 languages.

Don and his son Alex's 2016 book *Blockchain Revolution: How the Technology Underlying Bitcoin Is Changing Business, Money and the World* became the international bestseller on the topic. Harvard Business School's Clay Christensen identified it as *the* book "on how to survive and thrive in this next wave of technology-driven disruption." Don's TED Talk on the topic, "How Blockchain Is Changing Money and Business," has received over 5.9 million views on TED.com alone. In 2017, Don and Alex co-founded the Blockchain Research Institute, which has conducted over 100 projects investigating blockchain strategy, use-cases, implementation challenges, and organizational transformations. His advice is sought by business and government leaders in many countries.

Don graduated from Trent University in 1970 with a BA and Honours BSc in Psychology. Prior to becoming the chancellor, Don served as the chair of Trent's Beyond Our Walls fundraising campaign in the mid-1990s. In 2006, he was awarded an honorary degree by Trent for his accomplishments and service. In 2013 he became the first alumnus to hold the role of chancellor on the cusp of the university's 50th anniversary. I began my term as president in the following year.

The role of the chancellor includes conferring degrees and diplomas and sitting as an ex officio member of the Board of Governors and the Senate. In addition, the chancellor represents the university in an official capacity at many external functions. Each chancellor brings their own special talents and interests to the position, in a way that greatly enhances the life of the university.

As chancellor, Don presided over Trent's 50th anniversary celebrations, giving the keynote speech to the alumni reunion and symposium, speaking at the anniversary gala, and leading the community parade through the streets of downtown Peterborough. At the closing anniversary celebration, held at Showplace Theatre in downtown Peterborough, he reconstructed "Boys in the Band," his rock band that played at Trent and surrounding areas during his undergraduate days. They performed an updated version of Don's 1960s song "Morning Light," complete with hip hop sections, receiving a standing ovation from the capacity crowd.

During his six years as chancellor, Don presided over 47 convocation ceremonies and shook the hands of more than 7,200 students. He was a key speaker and host at the grand opening of the Student Centre and the transformed Bata Library. Other contributions to Trent included a lecture series, many presentations to Trent's students and the broader community at multiple venues, and international alumni gatherings, including events in New York and London, England. As chancellor he published numerous articles speaking to pertinent issues about higher education. He also participated in countless development and fundraising meetings and activities in support of the university.

While chancellor, Don moved up in the rankings of the Thinkers50 global ranking of management thinkers from ninth, to fourth, to second in 2017 and was recognized as the top Digital Thinker in the world in 2018. In 2016 Don received the Order of Canada for his leadership in the field of business innovation and the social impact of information technology.

Don proudly championed Trent wherever he went. Before and during his tenure, Don and his wife, Ana Lopes, continued to be generous donors to Trent. Thank you, Don, for your allegiance to Trent; for all you accomplished while serving as our chancellor; for your leading-edge thinking, sense of humour, and warm personality—and for the way you have inspired today's Trent students to follow in your footsteps and live a life of consequence.

# SPEECHES
# TO THE TRENT
# COMMUNITY

# CONVOCATION ADDRESS— HONORARY DOCTOR OF LAWS DEGREE

## The Value of a Liberal Arts Degree in an Ever-Changing World?

*Madam Chancellor, Madam President, graduates, friends, and family:*

Heartfelt congratulations to each of you graduating today and to those who share your success.

I'm deeply honoured and thankful to receive this degree. What profundities can I share to help you transition from this hallowed place back to your parents' basement?

To begin, I have a confession. Although I graduated from Trent, I never actually convocated. I loved my years at Trent—so much that I convinced my three younger brothers to attend. But I had no interest attending the ceremony, being too preoccupied with the challenges of stopping the war in Vietnam, supporting the women's rights movement, and in general organizing the world revolution for social justice and democracy. It was the 60s after all. In hindsight, I regret my decision. My heart might have been in the right place, but that was about all. So today, after waiting 35 years, my mother gets to attend the Trent Convocation

Ceremony and actually see me getting a degree. Thanks for being patient with me, Mom.

For many decades convocation speakers around the world have correctly told graduates how fortunate they are. And I would say the graduates here today are particularly fortunate. You are graduating from an outstanding university in the country that is consistently rated the best in the world to live in. And because you all chose Trent, you've all been involved—in varying degrees—in an interactive liberal arts and science experience. Trent insists all graduates take some liberal arts courses regardless of their chosen field. You should be thankful, since there is no better way to prepare yourself for work, lifelong learning, and citizenship in a knowledge economy.

Not everyone agrees with this view. Let me tell you a story. Several years ago, I chaired the Trent capital campaign. At the time there were newspaper articles, op-ed pieces, and government ministers saying we should cut back on liberal arts and focus on technical and training-oriented programs addressing specific needs of business. One piece said the BA was a "useless degree."

I discussed this issue over lunch one day in 2000 with Trent's chancellor, the late and dear Peter Gzowski. Together we hatched a plan to win the support of an influential and counterintuitive group: Canada's most senior high-tech CEOs. I asked the CEOs to attach their names to a public call for proper funding to liberal arts and science courses in Canadian universities. Of the 35 executives who received my email, 31 signed the statement within 48 hours.

The story was national news. One newspaper said it was actually no surprise the CEOs supported the public statement, since the majority of them had a liberal arts and science undergraduate education themselves! And the CEOs they interviewed were passionate about the issue, saying that their companies don't just need technical skills. If their companies were to prosper in an increasingly competitive marketplace, they needed people who could think, synthesize ideas, communicate, place things in context, and understand the relationship between things.

In this new world it's not just what you know that counts—it's your capacity to think and learn throughout your life, communicate, and, above all, collaborate.

Three decades ago, my generation entered the workforce with a base of knowledge and "kept up" in our chosen field. We thought we were set for life. Today you know this idea is laughable. Some of what you learned in your first year may already be obsolete. Your knowledge base is like software—and if you don't keep upgrading it, it won't be able to run in a digital enterprise.

Which is why a liberal arts education is so important. It helps you keep pace, understand, and react to the changes around you. Personally, I attribute much of whatever success I have had in the high-technology world to my liberal arts experience.

In psychology I learned about human motivation, personality, and cognition—the foundation of my work as a manager and teacher. The Sociology of Groups taught me to think in terms of teams and the dynamics of collaboration. From my small biology tutorial I learned (in addition to the importance of being prepared) the power of natural ecosystems—a concept applicable to just about everything. In English I developed my writing, and when my final essay was reduced from an A to a C (half a grade for each of four spelling mistakes), I developed attention to detail. There is nothing like history and anthropology to develop one's sense of context, and no one could excite a student about the power of the scientific method better than the late and great experimental psych prof Alan Worthington. A math teacher, Tom Nind, turned me on to computers in an after-hours programming group. I first read Thomas Kuhn at Trent—and the power of a paradigm, as mental model, still comes up weekly 35 years later. The enthralling Julian Blackburn taught me the importance of entertainment in teaching—people learn more when they are conscious. And the brilliant economics/sociology prof Pradeep Bandyopadhyay inspired the love of learning and empowerment that is in my bones today.

I'm sure each of you could tell a similar tale. Thus you are a graduating class uniquely significant and blessed—you've got a foundation for permanent learning.

Moreover, you have come of age in the digital age—with a global orientation, access to knowledge, collaborative spirit, innovative thinking, and a facility with the tools for learning and value creation that my generation could only begin to envy. You are uniquely equipped to lead this change. You've had the front-row seats on today's unprecedented upheaval. You've been studying it. And now you're moving onto the stage.

If you become a teacher, you won't be buried in a single school—you'll be able to collaborate with peers across the country. And your students will have access to virtually all recorded knowledge and expertise. As a business manager, you'll be working in corporate architectures dramatically different from those of the 20th century—ones that emphasize teamwork rather than hierarchy.

One chemistry major I met from this year's graduating class has already joined with 85,000 other chemists in the global InnoCentive network. He's now part of the virtual research and development (R&D) departments of Eli Lilly, Procter and Gamble and other companies. As a nurse, you can collaborate with colleagues around the world through myriad online communities, including ones populated by thousands of physicians and doctors—and not just keep up with the dizzying changes in your profession, but lead them.

Digital technologies are creating a world in which knowledge, power, and productive capability are more dispersed than at any time in our history—where value creation will be fast, fluid, and persistently disruptive—where only the connected will survive. A tough new business rule is emerging: collaborate or perish.

Evidence is growing that this may be the birth of a new era, perhaps even a golden one, on par with the Italian renaissance or the rise of Athenian democracy. Mass collaboration across borders, disciplines, and cultures is at once economical and enjoyable. We can collaborate to produce Linux, Wikipedia, blogs, mutual funds, and even physical things such as a motorcycle. The largest motorcycle maker is not a company—it's a self-organizing network of parts suppliers, builders, and distributors in China. They meet in tea houses and increasingly online to figure out how all their parts work together. Some companies make carburetors. Others do final assembly. The Chinese motorcycle industry is the Linux of the biker world.

Throughout most of history—and in much of the contemporary business world—the key players have perceived themselves as combatants in a zero-sum game. The fundamental motivation for investing in new skills and knowledge has been to do better at the expense of others. But as we transition to an economy based on non-rival knowledge and physical abundance, we must change our perceptions of the game. We must learn to recognize opportunities for mutually beneficial exchange, where our instincts may suggest competition. We must understand the principles of strategic collaboration.

As I said earlier, you are the vanguard of the first generation that intuitively understands the new economic framework. You have grown up in the digital era. I remember as a teenager emptying my piggybank to buy a 12-transistor radio at Eaton's. A single personal computer now contains a billion transistors. This year there were more transistors produced in the world than grains of rice—and at a lower cost. Reflect on that for a moment. And there is no end to such progress in sight. Transistors will continue to shrink, processor power will continue to double and redouble, chips will be imbedded into every object, Internet bandwidth will continue to expand, and if we will it, there will be far-reaching changes in the way we do business, work, play, take care of ourselves, and even think—for the better.

With this comes awesome responsibility. You also have a historic opportunity to create unprecedented progress in society and I'm not just referring to Canada or the wealthy nations. I ask that you listen to me with care:

A friend of mine, Riel Miller, who works for the OECD [Organisation for Economic Co-operation and Development], returned from a conference on the environment and asked me to guess the source of air pollution that killed the most people in the world. Perhaps you know the answer, but I didn't. I said cars, which was wrong, and then industrial emissions, which was also wrong, so then I gave up. The answer is cooking fires. Over a billion people cook in huts with no ventilation. And it is killing them.

According to the World Health Organization, more than two billion people live without basic sanitation. Over a billion people earn less than a dollar a day. To be sure, follow your dreams for prosperity as previous generations have done. But as a society we can't afford for you to do only that. We can't afford for you, as a generation, to disappear for the next 20 years as you build your businesses or advance your careers. We need you to apply the unique capabilities of your generation for the broader social good.

As a citizen you have at your fingertips the most powerful tool ever for finding out what's going on, informing others, and organizing collective responses. Corporations, governments, and other institutions are becoming naked—and if you're going to be naked, you'd better be buff. You are armed with knowledge, and knowledge is power. You have the power to change the world in ways that my generation did not. Network that knowledge and you can create a perfect storm for change.

Moreover, I believe you'll find that your personal goals for a good life will increasingly be linked to those of others on the planet. In this new world, self-interest and common interest are becoming aligned. Businesses need a world of social justice, equality of opportunity, and stability for an effective global marketplace for goods, services, and human capital.

My generation has not done the best job ensuring that your time has come. With you rest the hopes of the world. Carry this mantle well.

# CONVOCATION ADDRESS—CHANCELLOR INSTALLATION

## The Age of Collaboration

*Mr. President, graduates, friends, and family:*

Heartfelt congratulations to each of you graduating today and to those who share your success.

I am deeply honoured to have been chosen as the 11th chancellor of Trent University and I'm humbled knowing what large shoes of former chancellors I have to fill. I've also been looking forward to my installation today with great anticipation.

The word "installation" is an interesting one, causing me to reflect on what else we "install." Air conditioners? Sinks? Light fixtures? Carburetors? The main thing that gets installed in my world is software. So think of me as the Trent 11th Chancellor App. Today is my official booting up. You don't even need to read the installation manual because I'm now fully downloaded and ready to run. If I begin to slow down, you should feel free to demand a reboot or to recompile me. I'm hoping to serve you well and that I won't need an upgrade. But you never know—you may want a new version of me—let's call it Chancellor 2.0. (Well, those of you who studied computer science may have found that funnier than the rest of you.)

In seriousness, Trent has always been a very special place for me. As you know, Trent distinguishes itself through its focus on collaborative learning, where students not only receive information but work together to create and test new concepts.

I came to Trent because I wanted a personalized and interactive learning experience, and even back then Trent seemed to provide that. And it was a good choice. At Trent I wasn't just a passive recipient of knowledge but rather a co-creator of my own intellectual capacity.

You may not know it, but the Trent model of collaborative learning is in stark contrast to the models of the past. The industrial age was an age of standardization and scale, where something at the top pushed down standard units to passive recipients. Mass production. Mass media. Mass marketing. Mass education. Manufacturers, or journalists, or TV producers, or teachers pushed out standardized products, publications, shows, or lectures to audiences that were inert.

When it came to the university, learning was focused on the educator. The approach was the one-way lecture, one size fits all, and students were isolated in the learning process.

This is all changing. The Trent model is important because today's young students have grown up immersed in interactive media and communications, rather than being inert and isolated viewers of television like their boomer parents. As a result, they learn better through interaction and collaboration than being passive recipients.

Collaboration is important not just because it's a better way to learn. The spirit of collaboration is penetrating every institution and all of our lives. So learning to collaborate is part of equipping yourself for effectiveness, problem solving, innovation, and lifelong learning in an ever-changing networked economy.

The digital revolution has distributed knowledge and enabled new models of working and learning together. We're entering a new age of participation, where collaboration is spreading across the world like a prairie fire and teams are critical to almost everything. Rather than superiors and subordinates, peers can now come together to do almost everything—sometimes on an astronomical scale. Thousands of volunteers have collaborated in creating Linux, the world's most important computer operating system. Hundreds of thousands of amateur astronomers are mapping the heavens as part of Galaxy Zoo. Millions of people have worked together to create Wikipedia, an encyclopedia that is in 240 languages and (according to the biggest study) has the same error rate as *Britannica*. Hundreds of millions of people have joined Facebook Causes, each looking for ways to work with others to build a better world.

This is so important for the different faculties in the audience today.

Those of you graduating in Business Administration will be successful through collaborative approaches rather than traditional command-and-control hierarchies. Procter and Gamble now gets 60 per cent of its innovations by finding the uniquely qualified minds for discovery outside the walls of the company. Companies turn their customers into producers or "prosumers" like Threadless, a clothing company where the customers design the clothes. The Chinese motorbike industry is made up of dozens of small companies that work together, with no overall motorcycle company pulling the strings. This is now 40 per cent of the world's motorcycle production.

Some of you will be entrepreneurs or join small companies, and collaboration opens a world of new possibilities for you. Small companies can now have all the capabilities of large companies without all the liabilities—legacy cultures, systems, and processes. Because of the Internet, talent can now be outside a company's boundaries and customers inside. More and more, society will create wealth through networks of collaborators rather than industrial-age behemoths (a word I learned, by the way, studying sociology at Trent).

This is so important because, among other reasons, 90 per cent of new jobs in Canada come from companies five years old or less. If we're ever to overcome the so-called jobless recovery, entrepreneurship and collaboration will be the key.

In addition to getting their great innovations from networking with talent outside their boundaries, big companies benefit from entrepreneurship too, as many are acquiring brilliant small companies with great innovations rather than relying solely on their research and development departments. As the new saying goes M&A (mergers and acquisitions) is the new R&D (research and development).

If you're graduating in nursing, your working life will be one of collaboration, as nursing has changed from being an occupation to a full profession in its own right; health care itself is being transformed. Nurses are now truly at the heart of patient care. As nurses, you will be working in interdisciplinary, collaborative teams that involve doctors, social workers, research clinicians, therapists, educators, administrators, and the patients themselves. These teams design and execute a complete wellness program for a patient in the context of their whole life.

Collaborating with patients is something new. The industrial model of health care—as with media, production, education, and everything else—clinicians delivered care to passive recipients. ("I'm a clinician. I have knowledge. You're a patient. You don't. I deliver health care to you.") I remember after I graduated from Trent, asking our family doctor a question during a diagnosis. He answered that he was the doctor and he would do the questioning. How things have changed since then!

Today patients are informed like never before. Moms are checking their kids' symptoms on the Mayo Clinic's website. Millions of people with various disorders are learning from each other on platforms such as PatientsLikeMe.com. As an example, 20 per cent of all North Americans with Lou Gehrig's disease (ALS, amyotrophic lateral sclerosis) are learning from each other's experience there. And clinicians and medical researchers are huge beneficiaries.

In fact, health research is changing too. The pharmaceutical companies this year are losing a quarter of their revenue due to something called the patent cliff—whereby many blockbuster drugs are losing their patent protection. They have no choice but to reinvent their industry by sharing clinical trial data. Imagine how sharing medical research data in a commons could not just transform the industry but lead to breakthroughs in human health.

Collaboration will affect all of you in another way—as citizens. Trent describes itself as the champion of collaborative learning that is personal, purposeful, and transformative. Many of you came to Trent because you care and want to make a difference, not just in your profession but in the world. And this is a time of great transformation. My hope is that you will be not only effective professionals but agents for change in these troubled times.

I'm sure it's no revelation to you that our society has many problems. Youth unemployment everywhere is high. Many of the institutions of the industrial age that have served us well for decades, from old models of the corporation, media, government, science, the financial services industry, seem paralyzed and unable to move forward. Leaders of institutions everywhere have lost trust. The global economy is stalled and the world is deeply divided, too unequal, unstable, and unsustainable.

Your generation will need to turn this situation around—find new solutions for our connected world—and each of you will have a role to play. You will need to participate in change in your workplace, community, country, and in causes you join, as a global citizen. And you will need to teach your children well.

I believe that you are uniquely equipped to lead this change. As you enter the workforce and society, you will have at your fingertips the best tools ever for innovation, patient care, research, and learning. And your Trent experience will serve you well.

As citizens, I hope you will demand more transparent government and that politicians engage with you more than simply asking for your vote. I'm hopeful that you'll bring about a whole new era of democracy. The first wave of democracy established elected and accountable institutions of governance, but with a weak public mandate and an inert citizenry. You can bring in a second wave, characterized by strong representation and a new culture of public deliberation built on active citizenship.

I'm not suggesting that each of you become a candidate for prime minister or world leader. Change will happen in every home, community, business, hospital, clinic, organization, and every nook and cranny of society. It's an opportunity if you want it.

Wherever you are, design your life. Live the values of your generation. Continue your university experience with a full life that is purposeful, transformational, and consequential.

Like you I'm embarking on a new role. You're becoming alumni and I'm becoming a chancellor. I'm excited about intensifying my collaboration with Trent—but only if you, the faculty, students, and alumni want me to.

Your time has come. The hopes of the world rest with you. Carry this responsibility well. Remember, you never carry it alone.

(And hey, if you want to collaborate with me, I'm @dtapscott on Twitter. Or connect with me on LinkedIn. Or friend me on Facebook.)

# CONVOCATION ADDRESS

## Designing Your Life

*Mr. President, Ms. Chairman of the Board, graduates, friends, and family:*

Heartfelt congratulations to each of you graduating today and to those who share your success. It's usually the job of convocation speakers to give inspiring, motivational thoughts for the next stage of your life.

But I'm not really a motivational speaker. So I'd like to do the only thing I know how—share some thoughts about the real world you're entering and give you a few provocative ideas for you to think about.

The occasion of Trent's 50th anniversary caused me to reflect about how the world has changed over the last half century for graduates. You'll find this hard to believe judging by my youthful appearance, but I have some first-hand experience—as I started Trent in 1966. Some of you who are computer science grads will know that there was not a single computer at Trent. There was no mobile web in the workplace because there was no web (that was 25 years later) and no mobility (all telephones were connected with a wire to a wall so people could only call you at your desk—I miss that). The metabolism of innovation was glacial, and we went to the Canadian National Exhibition (CNE) each year to see this year's innovation. Work, careers, relationships, life was blissfully simple compared to today.

The pace and complexity of existence today are creating a new imperative: it makes sense to design your life, in ways that my generation never had to.

Let's look at three aspects—your life as a learner, a professional, and a citizen.

## 1. Design your strategy for lifelong learning

My colleagues and I entered the workforce with a base of knowledge and "kept up" in our chosen field. We thought we were set for life. Today you know this idea is laughable. If your degree only marked a milestone in your knowledge, you'd be set for (to use Andy Warhol's aphorism) about 15 minutes. Much of what you learned in your first year is obsolete.

I know you're celebrating a milestone today, but don't think that your higher education is completed. It has just begun.

Lifelong learning is an assumption for you; you'll need to reinvent your knowledge base multiple times as you go through life. And as graduates from a liberal arts and sciences university, you know that it's not just your knowledge that's important. It's your ability to think, collaborate, solve problems, synthesize, and to learn and learn again, again, and again.

Furthermore, in a knowledge economy, working and learning are almost indistinguishable as activities. When you begin your first job what will you be doing—working or learning?

This raises some interesting imperatives for you:

- **Bake learning into work in innovative ways.** Don't take the "best" job offer based on traditional criteria like how much it will pay. Select a job that maximizes your opportunities for learning. The cash will get lost in the rounding figure of your lifelong income and fulfillment. Look for ways to increase the learning components of your work. Seek assignments that are not only interesting or where you can make contributions but where you can learn the most. And design your own professional development program where you can advance your knowledge in important new ways outside of work. MOOCs (massive open online courses) will be a godsend for you here.

- **Design your media diet.** When I graduated, there were several TV stations and newspapers that we all relied on and we could trust the Columbia Broadcasting System's Walter Cronkite to tell the truth.

  Today you have millions of choices for where you get your information. You need to develop your BS detectors and make choices about how you will interact with this avalanche of information. Be skeptical, not cynical about what you read and see. The antidote to information overload is to develop your personal filters. And don't just skim—read at least a couple of articles from beginning to end every day.

- **Increase your formal learning.** Get a diploma or an additional degree. In the old economy an undergraduate degree was enough. Perhaps not now. During the Industrial Revolution the leaders of society understood that the population needed to be literate, and everyone had to go to school. What is the equivalent for the knowledge economy? Most people will need higher education, and for the leaders one degree will not be enough.

## 2. Design your vocation

I'm sure it's no revelation to you that you are entering the next stage of your lives in troubled times. Youth unemployment everywhere is high, and many refer to the jobless recovery—an oxymoron if ever there was one. There is no recovery unless it's inclusive.

You have no need for despair or even worry. Research shows that nearly all of you will get jobs and most of them will be related to your major field of studies. It may take a little longer compared to 50 years ago, but it will happen.

However, the world has changed in other ways since I graduated. Back then most students wanted to work for a big company like IBM, General Motors, a consulting company, big bank or to get a job as a teacher or government employee. Today these options are less feasible as hiring has declined.

However, there are new choices and a big one is to be an entrepreneur. Research shows that most new jobs come from relatively new companies. Entrepreneurship is the key to jobs.

There is a lesson here for you. Look for opportunities to join small companies, not just big organizations. Or do the unthinkable. Explore the idea of creating your own business. Small companies can now have all the capabilities of large companies without all the liabilities—legacy cultures, systems, and processes. Because of the Internet, talent can now work outside a company's boundaries and customers can contribute inside. Increasingly, society will create wealth through networks of collaborators rather than industrial-age corporations.

This doesn't mean throw caution to the wind and get your parents to mortgage their house to fund your big idea. Typically it makes sense to get some work experience and to develop an idea, a business plan, and the connections to make it happen. But you might be one of the new generation of business builders who will make a real difference in achieving prosperity in Canada. Or by being a social entrepreneur, you can do well by doing good in the world at the same time. Which brings me to my final point.

## 3. Design your life as a citizen

Today your degree from Trent equips you well for thinking, collaborating, researching, solving problems, and lifelong learning. So as you leave these hallowed halls, by all means (as Spock would say), "Live long and prosper." Build a successful and prosperous life for yourselves and your families.

But let me argue that humanity needs more of you. Fifty years ago there was plenty of upheaval in the world with big movements for civil rights, women's rights, and against the war in Vietnam.

If the 60s were a turning point in history, they pale in comparison to the challenges facing your generation. You are being called upon to fix a broken world, the one that my generation is leaving you. (Sorry about that).

So my hope is that you will each design your life to be a consequential one—beyond your vocation. Today's global economic malaise is symptomatic of a world with big challenges. Many of the institutions that have served us well for decades—even centuries— seem frozen and unable to move forward. The global economy and financial services industry, governments around the world, health care systems, newspapers, the media, and our institutions for solving global problems like the United Nations are all struggling. Our energy and transportation systems are spewing enough carbon to threaten our biosphere.

The world is becoming even more unequal, unstable, and unsustainable. At the annual Davos meeting of the World Economic Forum this year, Bill Clinton gave evidence to a group of us that if we reduce carbon emissions by 80 per cent in the year 2050, it will take a thousand years for the world to cool down. In the meantime, bad things are likely to happen—like 1.5 billion people will lose more than half of their water supply.

Your generation will need to turn this situation around to rebuild our institutions and the world.

Now don't get me wrong. I'm not suggesting that each of you work for an NGO (nongovernmental organization) or become a candidate for the leader of the world or something like that. Rather, each of you will have a role to play in this historic transformation whether you are an entrepreneur, consultant, business executive, educator, researcher, public sector manager, politician, social innovator, or parent. It's an opportunity for each of you if—you will it.

You will need to participate in change in your workplace, community, country, causes you join, and as a global citizen. And you will need to teach your children well.

One simple thing you can do is to just vote! All around the world young people are cynical about our political institutions. And justifiably so—from the mayor of Toronto to the paralysis of the US Congress—"Something Seems Rotten in the State of Democracy." Although young people care about the future and are active in achieving change, youth voting is on a precipitous decline across the Western world. More and more of you agree with the bumper sticker "Don't vote, it only encourages them." This is leading to a crisis of legitimacy of our democratic institutions.

But don't give up on democracy. The alternatives for you, your future families, and loved ones are not desirable. So I encourage you to be a political person—with a small P—for starters by voting in every election that comes along. Please don't ever, ever miss voting in an election at the local, provincial, or federal level.

Canada needs your good judgment, critical thinking, passion, and demographic muscle to ensure that this smaller country your children inherit is a better one.

I have never been more optimistic about the future because I believe we are in the early days of a new civilization—one that is enabled by a communications revolution and forged by young people around the world. Because each of you can participate in this new renaissance, it is surely an amazing time to graduate and to be alive.

I hope you will have the wisdom and the will to seize the time and design your life to make it work for you and for our collective future.

Godspeed to each of you.

# IDEAS THAT CHANGE THE WORLD SYMPOSIUM— KEYNOTE ADDRESS
## 50th Anniversary Event

*First of all, let me begin by saying that I'm delighted to be here. I really mean that. I've had my share of appointments, jobs, accolades, and so on over the years, but I've never been more delighted or proud than to be the first alumni chancellor of Trent University.*

The theme of this symposium is about ideas that change the world—and we have a world that needs changing, surrounded by technological wonders and miracles, new advances in science, the development of global supply chains, our productive capacity. We're facing a situation where many things are deteriorating in the world. We have growing social inequality all across the Western world. We have structural unemployment. We've got a world that's unsustainable. We are destroying our environment, and climate change threatens to extinguish many species, including ours. And conflict is growing. So we need to bring about change.

This symposium, "Ideas That Change the World," has five themes—education, life and health, critical cultural inquiry, Indigenous people, and sustainability and the environment. What I'd like to do is to introduce some ideas on each of these.

First, on education, the model of pedagogy we use in our schools and universities is an appropriate one for the 17th century but is inappropriate for today.

Second, on life and health, we need to change the whole paradigm for how we deliver health care and how we do medical research, moving to a collaborative model.

Third, there's a fragmentation of public discourse, in large part because of the digital media. How do we overcome that?

Fourth, all of us are deeply concerned, even shocked, by the chronic injustices and situation facing Indigenous peoples. One of many questions is how do we overcome the problem of unemployment in these communities? I'm going to make the case that entrepreneurship is going to be the key. And the Internet can help us big time.

Fifth, to reverse the trend of climate change, we need to govern the climate. More specifically, what the world needs now is a global governance network, similar to the ecosystem that governs the Internet. If we can govern a resource like the Internet through a rag-tag community of people and different stakeholders, maybe we could govern other resources—one of them being the climate.

As many of you know, I've spent more than four decades thinking about the digital revolution and its impact on business and society. To me, this is the main driver for change. My book *The Digital Economy* was called the first bestseller about the corporation and business. Unbelievably, that was in 1994. Back then the world was very different. We accessed the web through dial-up, remember that? Google wasn't to come into the marketplace for five years; there was no Amazon; there was no eBay.

Well, flash-forward to today. And we've got an unbelievable explosion that's occurring. We've got the social web that connects more than 3.9 billion people in real time. We have the rise of big data.

And I think that the owners of big data are creating new empires of wealth that may far exceed previous empires we've known, based on other resources like minerals or oil or power over people, or even financial capital. This is a new form of capital that's emerging.

We've got the rise of the so-called Internet of everything where billions and trillions of inert objects in our world become smart communicating devices. I have a friend in Toronto whose house is a good example—everything in it that has electrical power has an IP address. That means that they're connected to the Internet and all these things talk to each other. I have no idea what his toaster says to his refrigerator, but he was actually bragging that his fence talks to a sprinkler system. And I said, "Ken, why would you care," and he said, "Don, if a burglar comes over the fence, the sprinkler is my first line of defence."

We've got pervasive mobility. We're connected at all times. And this is an extraordinary thing. What it's doing is taking us into the second half of the chess board—do any of you know this analogy?

The inventor of chess was called into the Chinese emperor's palace. And the emperor said, and I paraphrase, "I love this game, you can have anything you want." And the inventor said, and I paraphrase, "Cool. I would like a single grain of rice on the first square of the chess board. And I'd like two grains of rice on the second square and four grains of rice on the third square. And just continue that." And the emperor, figuring this is a few bags of rice, said, "Are you sure?" And the inventor said yes. Two days later, the emperor had done the math and figured out that every square inch of planet Earth would need to be covered by rice fields to deliver on this wish.

And that's what's happening with the digital revolution. The last 25 years was the first half of the chess board. And we're now moving into a period where technology is accelerating at a rate that's so fast I think it's beginning to move beyond our ability as individuals, as institutions, and as societies, to even comprehend it—let alone to manage it and exploit it effectively.

And this is taking us into a new period in human history. I think that the Industrial Revolution is finally coming to a logical end, and we are moving into a digital age of networked intelligence. If you look around today, you'll see a whole set of institutions that are in various stages of being stalled or frozen, or even failing. That contrasts with a set of sparkling new initiatives that show how this could be done very differently.

Our models of solving global problems are universities and schools. All of these are based on an industrial model where something at the top pushed out standard units to passive recipients. The industrial age was an age of scale and of standardization. We pushed out newspapers, products, radio shows, government services, lectures, one too many, one size fits all, you're inert. Well, now we're moving into a new period where we have a new age, an age of networked intelligence.

Before I get into the five themes, let me flash back in a typical Trent way and look at the really big picture here. And we'll go back a few centuries. All around the world, we had an industrial age; the means of production and political system was called feudalism. And knowledge was tightly concentrated in tiny oligopolies of the church and the state. And people didn't have knowledge, really. They didn't know about things. There was no concept of progress, you were just sort of born, you lived your life, and you died.

Then along came Johannes Gutenberg with his great invention. And over time, people in different parts of the society began to acquire knowledge. And when they did, the institutions of feudal society appeared to be stalled or frozen or in atrophy or even failing. It didn't make sense for the church to be responsible for medicine when people had knowledge. Martin Luther called the printing press God's highest act of grace. So we saw the rise of science, the corporation, the modern university, all these new institutions, and it was good. But it did come with a cost.

And now once again, the technology genie is out of the bottle. Only this time it's very different. The printing press gave us access to the written word. The Internet enables each of us to be a publisher. The printing press gave us access to recorded knowledge. The Internet gives us access to knowledge—and to the intelligence contained in the cranium of other people—on a global basis. To me, this is not fundamentally an information age, it's an age of networked intelligence. It's an age of vast new opportunity and promise.

But when you look around today, many of the promises are not being fulfilled. Why don't we have growing prosperity? How can we be in a period of history where growth in the economy does not create growth in jobs? How can social inequality be growing? So we need some ideas to change the world.

## Rethinking Education

We no longer have an economy where we create wealth by brawn. Increasingly, we create wealth by brain. Knowledge work is becoming central to the entire economy in many, many ways. This is one of the arguments for our needing a liberal arts education. Because when I graduated from Trent in 1970, we—and I'm speaking as a white man of European descent—we sort of chose a field and we kind of kept up, and we were pretty much set for life. Today, graduates know they're not set for life. They're set for like—I don't know—15 minutes.

The purpose of education to me is not to equip or train young people for their next job. The purpose of education is to enable them to think, to think critically. Not just to be good employees to meet labour market demands, but to be good citizens for a world that's in transformation. So graduates today from Trent know that they're going to have to reinvent their knowledge base.

So if that's the purpose of education, how can we have a model of pedagogy that enables that purpose to be achieved? Well today, the model of education is the industrial-age model. It's based on the lecture. Everyone's passive in the learning experience. It's like, I'm a teacher and I have knowledge. You're a student and you don't. Get ready, here it comes. Now, I appreciate the irony that I'm standing up here giving you a lecture. But this is actually not a good way of learning.

Lectures are good for motivating people, but there are better models of pedagogy that are possible today. The old ways focused on the teacher. It's one way, it's one size fits all. And the student's isolated. There's a new model that's emerging, that's centred on the student, that's multi-way, that's customized, and that's collaborative.

Where there's a right or wrong answer, all the research shows that the best way to learn that is interactively through software on a computer. When I did my master's degree in education at the University of Alberta in 1975, I took a statistics course in a computer lab. I went through this stuff at my own pace, taking and retaking tests. I remember thinking, wow, if people saw me going over this again and again, they'd think I was really dumb. But nobody saw me. I went over it until I mastered it. There were no lectures, but let's face it, the statistics lecture by definition is a bust, right? I mean, everyone is either bored or doesn't get it. I ended up being really good at statistics and getting a graduate degree in research methodology. I even won the big scholarship for the university. I thought, wow, five years from now, lectures will be gone. That was 1975.

You master skills in a flipped classroom from your dorm room or your own home. You do the really important stuff—such as arguing a point, solving problems as a team, or standing up for others in the classroom. A teacher's role doesn't become less important; it becomes more important. This is because it frees up teachers from being transmitters of data to doing what only teachers can do, which is to work with people as individuals. So you have small-group discussions along the model of Trent. And you have projects where you learn.

Consider a company called Knix Wear. When my daughter did her graduate degree, an MBA at INSEAD outside Paris, she had to create a business plan. She and her best friend, Joanna Griffiths, thought up a business that would reinvent women's underwear. They created an idea for a company and there was a big competition, 45 teams. They ended up winning. They launched it, grew it, created jobs, and went on to lead other innovations and manage larger teams. They learned more in that project than they could have in a lifetime of sitting passively in a lecture theatre.

If we had schools like Amherst College, where my son went for his undergraduate degree, you wouldn't need any technology, really. Class size ratio of eight to one, 1,600 students, and an endowment of $1.6 billion, which I think is bigger than the University of Toronto. And he was sitting there in a class with eight students and his prof who won the Pulitzer Prize for his book on Russia. And they're all interacting and that's it. It was like Trent—when I went to Trent, my biology seminar was me and the prof. Who's done their homework? Who'd like to answer this question?

Through the effective use of technology, we can reinvent that. You see, Trent was always about learning that's purposeful, that's personalized, that's collaborative, and that's transformational. And that's why I went to Trent. And Trent attempts to achieve that today. But I'm arguing that you can't achieve that unless you aim the mastery part at the year 2030 or 2050.

In 2008, I was invited to Florida State University to spend a very long lunch with the university's deans and management. They were doing a billion-dollar fundraiser, and they wanted to create the first 21st-century university. They were asking my view on what that was. I explained that my generation grew up being the passive recipients of TV, and sitting in on a lecture hall was the right model of learning for me. But kids today have grown up interacting, and we have an opportunity to reinvent the university pedagogy, the relationship between the university and other institutions in society. At the end of my talk, I got a little applause, very tepid.

There was a young person in the room, 22 years old, named Joe. A dean said, "Joe, you're the one student here, why don't you start off the discussion?" And Joe said, "I've been reflecting on this and it's relating to me. I think actually as a generation, we probably do learn differently. For example, I don't read books. I go onto the Internet to find information and knowledge, and I've got a pretty good bull s— detector to know what's good and what's not good. If I have to read a whole book, I don't follow someone's narrative. I'm bouncing around. I'm on the net, I'm into the index and the table of contents. And I'm coming back and checking on stuff. I don't read books."

I said to Joe, "Tell me about yourself." He said—and I'm para-phrasing here—"I'm a good student." I said, how good? He said, "I've always had As, a 4.0 grade average." I said, "Did you do anything else here?" He said, "Well, I'm the president of the student council. I manage a budget of $12 million, and I'm on 18 committees. I chair 11 of them and that takes some time." And I said, "I'm sure it does."

"Do you do anything else?" He said, "Well, usual sports stuff. The really big thing was during my first year. Hurricane Katrina hit and my girlfriend is from New Orleans. So we went down there to see if we could help. There was no health care clinic in the devastated Ninth Ward so I set one up." I said, "You set up a health care clinic?" He says, "Yeah, if you have the Internet, you can do anything you want."

I said, "What are you doing next year?" He said, "I'm going to Oxford. I'm doing a master's in philosophy." And I said, "That's great, Joe. I mean, did you get some financial aid?" He said, "Oh yeah, I got a Rhodes scholarship. It's great. It's going to cover everything."

The Rhodes scholar, in Florida in 2008, doesn't read books. So this is a time of profound change and we need to listen to the students. The most powerful force for change in schools and the universities is the students. This is the first time in history when the young people are an authority on something really important and they can teach us so much.

## Rethinking Health Care

We have an industrial-age model of health care. I'm a clinician. I have knowledge. You're a patient. You don't. I deliver health care to you. You're a nerd and passive in this process. Please don't go on the Internet because you'll get a lot of garbage and don't collaborate with anyone else because you're going to get all confused. One way, one size fits all. I got control. I got the knowledge. I deliver it to you. You're inert in the experience.

What's the new model? There's an environment called "Patients Like Me" created by a guy whose brother had ALS. And today, 20 per cent of all people with ALS in North America collaborate on this environment. They learn from each other. They understand the impact of drug interaction. Someone discovers this or that, or a diet thing. Clinicians love this because it's generating all this knowledge about the disease; Patients Like Me is now getting into all kinds of different diseases and disorders, including psychiatric disorders like depression.

So could we move toward this little tip of the iceberg of a whole new paradigm? Here it is. That you participate in health communities, and every baby in Canada gets a website when they're born, their personal web page, and we all get one too. It's half your electronic health care record, it's private and secure. The clinicians provide the data, but you have transparency into your own record. And it's also a social network for health. So if you have diabetes, you go into a diabetes community or you create one. It's just like Facebook: you come in in the morning and there's a newsfeed and you get to input information. This would generate massive data that could be transformative for medical research. Health care professionals could change from being the deliverers of health care to people who curate healthy citizens, rather than just patients. You look at something like obesity, a huge problem. How are we going to fix this? By telling people they shouldn't eat so much?

Isolation is the number-one risk factor in health. Imagine if people who had a weight problem could participate in communities. We know this works—Weight Watchers works. You build communities as opposed to the old industrial model where you delivered health care to passive recipients. This is a new model that embraces my five principles for transformation. It's about collaboration, openness, sharing data and information, integrity, and interdependence. Understanding that just like businesses can't succeed in a world that's failing, clinicians can't succeed in a world where we have massive social problems that are causing terrible health care outcomes.

Now let's apply this to research and health care. The model of health care research that we have today—I'm trying to be provocative here—is the antithesis of those five. You have researchers who compete for grants, and then they get the money and work together without collaborating. They don't share their data. They work in these little silos within universities and hospitals. And, sure, they're good people. They try to act with integrity, but it's doing the right thing for that institution, that hospital, that university, and building its reputation. It's not about trying to solve health care problems in the most effective way. So this is changing in many ways.

The pharmaceutical companies are falling over something called the patent cliff. What do you do? Cut back on office supplies? No, we need to change the model of pharmaceutical research. Pharmaceutical companies need to start sharing clinical trial data, and this is going to happen. We'll create a commons, a human genome of clinical trial data, a Linux of clinical trial data. Imagine how that's going to leapfrog health care research. Breakthroughs in medicine could be possible if we achieve this.

Will there be lots of problems to achieve this and research in general? Well, of course, but more and more people are saying this needs to be done. I'm on the research committee at the Centre for

Addiction and Mental Health, and Bruce Pollock, the VP of research, said real breakthroughs in discovering effective treatments of mental illness will occur when the silos within and between institutions doing research fall. We need to move to a new era of collaboration and the sharing of data and knowledge. Bruce said there hasn't really been a breakthrough in mental health research in more than 60 years. If you have schizophrenia today, you're getting the derivatives of the same medications that someone got 60 years ago. Why is this? Is the brain too hard to understand? Or is our model wrong?

Well, more and more people are saying our model's wrong. Trevor Young, the dean of the faculty of medicine at the University of Toronto, said there's a long tradition of sharing data and international collaboration on patient care and it works well. We need to apply that to discovery, and to research as well. So that's a big idea about transforming research. And when it comes to mental health research, this is beginning to happen. At the structural genomics consortium of people working together, the psychiatric genomics consortium is sharing all kinds of data, data sharing, data visualization, and open-source philosophy, and so on. Wow, if this can happen, it'll be a breakthrough. Welcome to the world of collaboration.

## Reclaiming Public Discourse

People like me have been saying that the Internet should advance public discourse. Imagine everyone, rather than passively receiving information controlled by broadcasters or their advertisers, having access to a world of information. All this rich data—surely the truth will set us free. We will move into a new period of better understanding of deep discussion, of great discourse, and where we can start to align together on all kinds of important initiatives that are required for society. The old media were centralized and controlled by their powerful owners. You know the old expression, the printing press was really a great idea, especially if you owned a printing press. The new media are the antithesis of all of that. It's not one to many, it's one to one, it's many to many, it has this awesome neutrality. It will be what we want it to be. Surely as a civilization, we will make it a platform for enriching ourselves and the way that we think. Billions of people are now collaborating on this platform.

The trouble is the evidence is that this thing I hope for, the digital economy 20-odd years ago, is happening in a very uneven way at best. And there all kinds of problems that are emerging. One of them is the so-called drowning in information. Eric Schmidt, Google's former executive chairman, said that between the beginning of time and 2003, humanity recorded five exabytes of information. That's a lot: an exabyte is a quintillion bytes. According to my math, in the last eight hours today, we recorded five exabytes of information. Now a lot of that is cat videos. But a lot of that is other stuff too. Do we have an information overload? Maybe we have a filter under-capacity.

In public discourse there's a real problem emerging whereby we're starting to see a fragmented conversation in the public world where you end up reinforcing your own points of view. Look at the United States today. There's a rise in anti-scientific thinking—for example, all kinds of people are not vaccinating their children. Concerning climate change, 99.9 per cent of the scientists in the world think that this is a really big problem, but there's a whole climate-change-denier industry. And it doesn't just come from vested interests. According to Paul Krugman, it comes from the rise of a new anti-intellectualism that exists in the United States. If knowledgeable and accredited and authoritative people say it, it must be wrong. We've got the rise of all these conspiracy theories, where you can google thousands and thousands of these wacko kinds of concepts that have come up.

Then we have the rise of new ideologies, everything from the Tea Party on the extreme right in the United States to very strong religious ideologies that exist all around the world. Many of these movements favour things like the elimination of public education and believe that women should be back in the home and barefoot. So is there a danger that we'll all end up in these self-reinforcing echo chambers where the purpose of information is not to inform us but to give us comfort? How do we overcome this problem? I interviewed a young woman on a panel once and she said, "I have newsfeeds that come to me from sources that I know I'm going to disagree with, but I want to hear them because I want to make sure I'm not wrong. And if I am right, I want to understand what the other point of view is saying to deepen my own thinking."

## Righting the Wrongs Done to Indigenous Peoples

Canada has a history of nothing less than genocide toward our Indigenous Peoples. The word *genocide* does not seem extreme if we consider the residential schools program. In Sir John A. Macdonald's words, its goal was to withdraw Indigenous children "as much as possible from parental influence" so they could "acquire the habits and modes of thought of white men." While the schools have been shuttered, the injustice continues, perpetrated by institutions in society and enshrined in the Indian Act.

One root cause is economic. If you look at data overall, unemployment among Aboriginal peoples varies from 12.7 per cent to 27.6 per cent across provinces and territories, and the rate is 10 per cent higher (19 per cent) than non-Aboriginal unemployment (9 per cent) in rural remote regions. Youth unemployment is easily double that.

How do we solve this problem? Here's an idea. Jobs. Do you know where jobs come from? Eighty per cent of new jobs come from companies that are five years old or fewer. According to David Newhouse, chair of Trent's Chaney Wenjack School of Indigenous Studies, there are already 26,000 Aboriginal entrepreneur companies in Canada. According to the Canadian Council for Aboriginal Business, a greater number of these Aboriginal businesses launch new products, services, or processes compared to Canada's small business sector overall, which suggests to me that they're more innovative. Could we move to a new halcyon day of Aboriginal entrepreneurship? Because the Internet enables little companies to have all the capabilities of big companies without the main bureaucracy, without the main liability.

How do we do that? Sixty per cent of Indigenous Peoples now live in cities, not on reserves. But on the reserves, there's a lot we could do and a lot's going on. I'll just tell you about one, called MentorNation, which is a community of mentors providing guidance, support, and assistance to entrepreneurs in Aboriginal communities. It went onto the Internet to raise some funds to do this. It was a very cool thing. Lots of people took on a target. I took on a target that I would raise $4,000. Then I sent out emails to everybody I know saying contribute along with me to this. Through this process, they raised close to $100,000 crowdfunding to provide these mentorships for entrepreneurs in Aboriginal communities. Go to MentorNation, have a look, and see what you think. And maybe you could personally contribute. Every one of the people who volunteered to raise some money (as I did) got their own little video. So when my friends go there and make a donation, it says how much they donated, if they want it to, with a little picture of them. Or they can even have their own little video on why they made this donation as well. This is using the Internet for good. A tiny step forward, but such steps add up.

## Governing the Climate

Do I have to convince anyone here that climate change is a big problem? Bill Clinton, at Davos, said if we reduce carbon emissions by 80 per cent in the year 2050, and we need to do that—if we do it by 80 per cent, it'll still take a thousand years for the planet to cool down. In the meantime, some bad things are going to happen. He said we can expect a billion and a half people to lose at least half of their water supply in the next decade. Elizabeth Kolbert, the author of *The Sixth Extinction*, said we're going through one of these extinctions right now, like the dinosaur extinction, but the scientists differ on how many species will be wiped out in the next hundred years. The estimates range from 15 per cent to some saying 60 per cent. Interesting question, will bees be one of those? And of course, could humans be one of those as well?

So how are we going to fix this problem? Well, the old approach was that 44 countries met at Bretton Woods, New Hampshire, in 1944, to create the World Bank and the IMF. A year later, they created the United Nations, and a year later UN Educational, Scientific, and Cultural Organization (UNESCO) and the International

Organization for Standardization (ISO), and then the General Agreement on Tariffs and Trade (GATT) and the World Trade Organization (WTO) and the Group of Eight (G8) and the G20 global institutions—all based on nation-states. The trouble is the nation-state is kind of like the wrong size for a lot of these problems. And if you're a problem like climate change, you don't really know about nation-states, you're just a problem.

So is there a possibility of a new model emerging? Well, half of my time right now is exploring global solution networks, global networks that are, first of all, multi-stakeholder. They involve companies, civil society, organizations, NGOs, academics, foundations, governments, and individuals working together. They are addressing a global problem. They use a digital revolution to help them, and a state or a state-based institution does not control them. These networks are engaging tens of thousands of organizations and tens of millions of people on a daily basis. And nobody really knows about them. So how could we use these networks in solving the problem of climate change? It turns out there are 10 types of these networks, such as knowledge networks that create knowledge and advocacy networks that advocate for change. We've got operational and delivery networks. My daughter lived in New York City when Hurricane Sandy hit. She couldn't find the traditional institutions, but she put out some tweets and people just showed up with sandbags. There are watchdog networks that scrutinize, there are standards networks that create standards, and so on.

Every one of these circles is kicking into action for climate change. And if you aggregate them all together, you're starting to see a network that could actually govern the climate. Knowledge networks like the climate and development knowledge network. They're just trying to better understand what's going on, what's happening to our biosphere. You've got operational and delivery networks that just kick in. They're not talking about it, they're not advocating, they're not creating knowledge, they just go into Honduras and clean up oil spills. You've got policy networks that are working on creating new policies. They're not controlled by states though. You've got advocacy networks that are collaborating and advocating that governments need to change.

We've got watchdog networks that are in the transparency business, just scrutinizing what's happening today to the climate and its impacts. For example, AVAAZ, a nonprofit activist organization, is enabling others to self-organize around all sorts of issues. There are global standards networks creating all kinds of standards around carbon. There are network institutions like the World Economic Forum, the Clinton Global Initiative, and so on that are doing all kinds of things in tackling this issue. What if we put them all together? Could we create a governance network? We need a governance network that involves all these different stakeholders and that can mobilize the world.

We've been mobilized before as a civilization in the first and second world wars, but we were on different sides. Now we need to mobilize the world so that we're on the same side, every company and every government at every level, every NGO, kids in their schoolyards, families taking on quotas. It turns out the killer app for the Internet may be saving the planet literally.

## Leadership for Change

In closing, this is a time of great change. I'm hoping that the discussion today will be a rich one and that we won't just be tinkering with how could we fix this or tweak that or so on, but that we'll be exploring very fundamental change in each of these five areas. I've attempted to describe five big ideas on these five topics.

I started out on sort of a depressing note: Will the future be a bleak one? Well, to me the future is not something to be predicted. It's something to be achieved, and we can achieve a very different future than the future that appears to be emerging for us. If we're going to do that, we need some big ideas and we need to all get involved. If we do that by the tens and hundreds of millions, then maybe this smaller network world that are our children inherit will be a better one.

I'm going to end with a sort of chancellor thought. And it's sort of a personal confession that when I left Trent, I lost contact with the university for a long period. People like Tony Story, head of Alumni Relations, kept sending me emails. And I kept saying, why is this guy sending me emails? And it was a couple of decades later that I decided to get involved again. I ended up chairing the capital campaign for Trent and I became an active alumnus. And I did that not out of a sense of obligation or a sense that there might be some personal benefits for me in being part of this community, which of course there are, but out of a sense that this institution is worth defending and it's worth preserving and advancing. And that the DNA of Trent is the DNA of the 21st-century educational institution. And that I have an opportunity as an alum to participate in ensuring that this institution thrives for the next period. So I hope that all of you who are alumni will come to the same conclusion. If this is the first time you've had contact with the university—and there are a lot of people out there in cyberspace watching this—you might think, yeah, maybe there's a role for me in participating in this community to help change a world that does need changing. Thank you very much.

# CONVOCATION ADDRESS
## Thriving in the Digital Age

*Mr. President, graduates, friends, and family:*

Heartfelt congratulations to each of you graduating today and to those who share your success.

Convocation speeches like this are designed to inspire the graduating class and give some helpful ideas for the future. So let me dispense with that task quickly:

- Today is the first day of the rest of your life.

- Don't be discouraged. Turn lemons into lemonade. Winners never quit.

- Good things come to those that wait. And what doesn't kill you can only make you stronger.

- Buy a good suit, and more importantly a good shirt and good shoes. (Hello, it's all about the accessories!)

- Brush your teeth and floss (I can't over-emphasize the importance of flossing). Increase the proportion of vegetables in your diet, and (please) never show up for a job interview drunk!

There, that about sums it up. Are there any questions?

Seriously, Trent has always been a very special place for me. As you know, Trent distinguishes itself through its focus on collaborative learning, where students not only receive information but work together to create and test new concepts. Concepts like the fine art of essay procrastination, or how many weeks can a person reasonably avoid doing laundry before someone calls the cops?

I came to Trent because I wanted a personalized and interactive learning experience, and even back then Trent seemed to provide that. And it was a good choice. At Trent I wasn't just a passive recipient of knowledge but rather a co-creator of my own intellectual capacity.

You may not know it, but the Trent model of collaborative learning is in stark contrast to the models of the past. The industrial age was an age of standardization and scale—where something at the top pushed down standard units to passive recipients. Mass production. Mass media. Mass marketing. Mass education. Manufacturers, journalists, TV producers, or teachers pushed out standardized products, publications, shows, or lectures to audiences that were inert.

When it came to the university, learning was focused on the educator. The approach was the one-way lecture, one size fits all, and students were isolated in the learning process. They did, however, get some excellent REM sleep, which has a whole host of important health benefits. It was some of the most expensive sleep on the market, but anyway.

As a baby boomer, I was pretty comfortable with being the passive recipient of someone else's broadcasting. We boomers watched a lot of TV each day. I was told what to do by my parents. The org chart of the boomer family was Mom reported to Dad and the kids reported to Mom. I was kid number one of five so the dog reported to me. This hierarchy was enshrined in popular culture in shows like *Father Knows Best*. We went to church on Sunday where a minister broadcast to us. Companies pitch advertising to us—one way. My teacher broadcast to me at school. When I entered the workforce I had a boss who wanted to "supervise" me.

This is all changing. The Trent model is important because today's young students have grown up immersed in interactive media and communicating, rather than being inert and isolated viewers of television like their boomer parents. Over the years, we slowly figured out that we don't have to sit there and just watch the Toronto Maple Leafs lose in the playoffs—we can actually shriek directly into the television. What's more, the players will definitely hear us. Today's students learn better through interaction and collaboration than being passive recipients.

Collaboration is important not just because it's a better way to learn. The spirit of collaboration is penetrating every institution and all of our lives. So learning to collaborate is part of equipping yourself for effectiveness, problem solving, innovation, and lifelong learning in an ever-changing networked economy.

The digital revolution has distributed knowledge and enabled new models of working and learning together. We're entering a new age of participation, where collaboration is spreading across the world (kind of like measles in 2015) and teams are critical to almost everything. Rather than superiors and subordinates, peers can now come together to do almost everything—sometimes on an astronomical scale. Thousands of volunteers have collaborated in creating Linux, the world's most important computer operating system. Hundreds of thousands of amateur astronomers are part of Galaxy Zoo, where they're literally mapping the heavens—so at some point we should really stop calling them amateurs. Millions of people have worked together to create Wikipedia, an encyclopedia that is in 240 languages and (according the biggest study) has the same error rate as *Britannica*. Another interesting fact: the most visited page of all time is a tie between the entry for bacon and the entry for a book I wrote called *Wikinomics*. Hundreds of millions of people participate in networks (I call them global solution networks) that involve companies, governments at all levels, NGOs, academics, foundations, and individuals—all trying to make the world a better place.

That's not to say that there isn't a dark side to all this. Twenty years ago I wrote a book called *The Digital Economy*, which they say was the first bestseller about the web. I just published the 20th-anniversary edition and was forced to do a reality check on the digital revolution and what has occurred. I said this was a time of great promise but some bad things could occur.

## 1. "Dislocations in labour markets, with old industries and jobs disappearing."

Today: For the first time in history economic growth is not generating a meaningful number of new jobs. Young workers are taking the biggest hit. Google's former executive chairman Eric Schmidt said that job scarcity will be the biggest public policy issue for the next two or three decades. There are many causes but the biggest culprit is digital technologies. We've already seen knowledge work such as accounting and legal services being shipped offshore to cheaper employees. Soon the work will stay here but be done by computers. If you guys were graduating ten years from now, a computer named iChancellor would be giving this speech. Factor in the hangover from the financial collapse of 2008 and we're witnessing youth unemployment levels across the Western world from 15 to 60 per cent. This situation is not only immoral, it is creating a massive powder keg.

## 2. "The destruction of privacy in an unpreedented and irrevocable manner."

Today: This is a major topic on the minds of most thoughtful people. But since the book was written there has been profound change in how we need to safeguard privacy. So-called data minimization (limiting what information we give away) is no longer feasible. New approaches are required. I'd tell you what they are, but I have to protect my privacy. Sorry!

## 3. The Danger of "A Severe Bipolarization of Wealth."

Today: Income inequality is one of the hottest topics on the planet. It was listed as the number-one global risk by the World Economic Forum's 2014 meeting in Davos, Switzerland. It is the topic of the *New York Times* number-one best seller, *Capital in the 21st Century,* by the French economist Thomas Piketty. While many disagree with his socialist conclusions, Piketty's scholarship has been pretty much unassailable, showing that growing social inequality is endemic to capitalism, even in the digital age. And reasonably, people today are questioning whether the digital revolution might actually accelerate inequality.

## 4. "What impact will the digital economy have on quality of life?"

Today: This is a hotly debated topic and the jury is out. As for technology making us stupid, many measures of smartness (improving

IQ, standard test scores, university graduates, etc.) suggest otherwise. However, the quote from the brilliant Alan Kay in *The Digital Economy* seems prophetic: "Another way to think of roadkill on the information highway will be the billions who will forget that there are off-ramps to destinations other than Hollywood, Las Vegas, the local bingo parlour, or shiny beads from a shopping network!"

It will be up to your generation to reverse the dark side and ensure that the digital economy is one of promise fulfilled.

Today you're graduating from Trent with specializations in high-demand fields—chemistry, physics, computer science, geography, and psychology. (Psychology worked out pretty well for me.) And notwithstanding unacceptably high youth unemployment levels in Canada, you're probably thinking that you chose pretty well. And so you did. Employability in all these fields is high, and nearly all of you will find professional work related to your field of study within a year of graduating. But you may be surprised to know that so will your colleagues who are graduates in arts, humanities, and other so-called soft fields.

However, your generation is facing new challenges—and not just from the prospect of technology-induced structural deficiencies in labour markets. When I graduated, I thought I was set for life. Today, purely from the perspective of knowledge, you know that you're set for, say, 15 minutes. What's important is not just what you know, but your capacity to think critically, solve problems, collaborate, have passion, and learn lifelong—as each of you will need to reinvent your knowledge base again and again—some estimates say over seven times.

Some of you will be entrepreneurs or join small companies; collaboration opens a world of new possibilities for you. Small companies can now have all the capabilities of large companies without all the liabilities—legacy cultures, systems, and processes. Because of the Internet, talent can now be outside a company's boundaries and customers inside. Our society is beginning to create more wealth through entrepreneurial networks than through industrial complexes.

Eighty per cent of new jobs in Canada come from companies five years old or fewer. If we're ever to overcome the so-called jobless recovery, entrepreneurship and collaboration will be the key.

In addition to getting their great innovations from networking with talent outside their boundaries, big companies benefit from entrepreneurship too, as many are acquiring brilliant small companies with great innovations rather than relying solely on their research and development departments. As the new saying goes M&A is the new R&D. M&A is the new R&D. Write that down. If any of you goes on to work for Netflix, I've just given you a killer concept for a hit show. Literally dozens of people will watch it. Dozens!

Wherever you are, design your life, and I don't just mean your professional life. Design your media diet. One downside of the digital media is that it's causing a breakdown in public discourse. We can now follow our own point of view, and there is a danger that we'll all end up in some self-reinforcing echo chamber where the purpose of information is not to inform us but to give us comfort. Read the newspaper (online or otherwise). Don't just scan, read whole articles—including long articles. Listen to CBC (what's left of it, the Canadian Broadcasting Corp.). Develop your BS detectors because there is a lot of BS out there today.

Live the values of your generation. Well, except for the endless photos of your brunch on Instagram. Maybe leave just that one value behind. Develop your plan for lifelong learning. Continue your university experience with a full life that is purposeful, transformational, and consequential.

Collaboration will affect all of you in another way—as citizens. Trent describes itself as the champion of collaborative learning that is personal, purposeful, and transformative.

Many of you came to Trent because you care and want to make a difference, not just in your profession but in the world. And this is a time of great transformation. My hope is that you will not only be effective professionals but agents for change in these troubled times.

I'm sure it's no revelation to you that our society has many problems, as I've described above. Many of the institutions of the industrial age that have served us well for decades, such as old models of the corporation, media, government, science, the financial services industry, seem paralyzed and unable to move forward. Leaders of institutions everywhere have lost trust. The global economy is stalled and the world is deeply divided, too unequal, unstable, and unsustainable.

Your generation will need to turn this situation around. You'll need to find new solutions for our connected world—and each of you will have a role to play. You will need to participate in change in your workplace, community, country, causes you join, and as a global citizen. And you will need to teach your children well.

I believe that you are uniquely equipped to lead this change. As you enter the workforce and society, you will have at your fingertips the best tools for innovation, patient care, research, and learning ever. And your Trent experience will serve you well.

As citizens I hope you will demand more transparent government and that politicians engage with you more than simply asking for your vote or snort-laughing about your concerns about paying back student loans.

Now, I don't mean to put too much pressure on you guys, but I'm kind of pinning all my hopes on the fact that you'll bring about a whole new era of democracy never before experienced by mankind. The first wave of democracy established elected and accountable institutions of governance, but with a weak public mandate and an inert citizenry. You can bring in a second wave, characterized by strong representation and a new culture of public deliberation built on active citizenship.

I'm not suggesting that each of you becomes a candidate for prime minister or world leader. Change will happen in every home, community, business, hospital, clinic, organization, and every nook and cranny of society. It's an opportunity for each of you, if you will it.

# CONVOCATION ADDRESS

## Be Resilient and Recalibrate

*Mr. President, graduates, friends, and family:*

Heartfelt congratulations to each of you graduating today and to those who share your success. And special congratulations to those of you who are the first to achieve a university degree in your families. For sure a sign of the times and an indication about many great things in this country.

And I must say I am moved and humbled that the Trent community has decided to renew my role as chancellor for another three-year term. You may wonder what a chancellor does. I like the definition: "A Chancellor is like a bidet. Everybody likes to have one but no one really knows what they do." In my case, the role is more than ceremonial. I try to be helpful in any way I can. And it's been very rewarding for me.

I wanted to take these few minutes to share a very personal journey I've been though and draw some lessons from it.

As you probably know, writing books is central to my existence— as a profession but also as a way of bringing about change in the world. I've written 15 books and many of them have been impactful. As someone who is at the age where many people retire, I suppose as some point I should slow down.

Nevertheless, a little over two years ago I decided to take another kick at the can. The process works like this: authors work to come up with a good idea and then spend a lot of time writing a proposal. Your last publisher usually gets a first look and the rights to publish the book before others. Because I've got a great publisher, I always work hard to make a killer proposal and usually they jump at it and make me an offer I can't refuse.

In this case, I had a big idea. I collaborated with a colleague to create a book proposal about how the digital age had been captured by powerful forces, like big technology companies and financial services companies. The problem we identified was that despite the growth of wealth in our economies, social inequality is also growing, and for the first time in modern history prosperity is on the decline. Technology rather than being a solution was part of the problem.

We worked very hard on this over many months and finally with great excitement my agent submitted the proposal to my publisher in New York.

We were on pins and needles for several days as they read the proposal carefully and talked about it and finally they got back to us.

The CEO wrote: "I'm sorry to report that this isn't working for us. Not that the thesis is objectionable, it just isn't up to the standard of originality and clarity that has become Don's trademark. I wish I could offer something more constructive."

Really? A flat-out rejection. Thud. Over.

Honestly, I was seriously disheartened. In all my years I had never had a book proposal rejected.

"Well, they just don't get it," I thought. So my agent went out to the other top five publishers and shopped the book around. Every single one of them said they weren't interested.

At this point I was more than disheartened. I was shaken, confused, and after 35 years of successful book writing worried about my ability to figure out the next big thing. There seemed to be many younger thinkers emerging with fresh amazing ideas and I wondered if I should focus on less ambitious endeavours.

I decided to organize a father–son ski trip with my 28-year-old lad, Alex, who is an investment banker and technologist. On the chairlift and over dinner, we found ourselves talking a lot about the meaning of something completely different—digital currencies like Bitcoin—and at the end decided to work together on a paper on the topic. Our collaboration was enormously stimulating, and together we figured out that there was something very big going on here.

I decided, what the heck, let's take another kick at the can and do a book proposal together on this new topic. It was a risky thing, and I didn't want my first big professional experience with my son to be a bust. But we did it.

When our publisher read the proposal, they loved it and we had a publishing contract within days.

Then the hard work started. Of all the books I've written, this was the toughest. We interviewed 150 people and read everything written about the topic. We travelled around the globe meeting with people. Wrapping our heads around these ideas was so hard, and at times I was concerned that we'd bitten off more than we could chew. But I believed in myself and I shared that confidence with my son as best I could.

We were reminded of the old axioms. Genius is one part inspiration and 99 per cent perspiration. (Brings a whole new meaning to the one per cent problem.) We worked harder and it got more confusing. Every time we took a layer off the onion, there was another one. But we kept at it.

We spent last summer at the cottage and while everyone else was out on the dock or in a boat, we remained focused.

I remember in the 1960s during a psychology lecture at Trent given by the great professor Julian Blackburn, he described the "ah-ha" phenomenon. Together Alex and I had an ah-ha phenomenon. We concluded that the Internet is entering nothing less than a second era based on the underlying technology of Bitcoin—called the *block-chain*. For 40 years we've had the Internet of information; now we're seeing the rise of the Internet of value. The implications of this were staggering, we thought, and the writing began in earnest.

This technology, we decided, could help solve the prosperity paradox. It could be key to revitalizing culture. It could enable billions of people to be part of the global economy. We realized that we were investigating a new possible future for civilization.

When the summer was over, we had a manuscript and sent it to the publisher. To say they were thrilled would have been an understatement. We spent the next four months reworking sections, fact checking, and adding in new material, and early this year sent it out to reviewers.

The book came out a month ago, and to my relief it got some pretty sweet reviews. We got words like "masterpiece" and "iconic book of our time." Within a week, it was the third best-selling book in the United States. Damn you, Harry Potter. And who ever heard of an adult colouring book anyway!

Which brings me back to you, dear graduates.

Of course you have big challenges ahead. The data shows you will each find work and it will be related to your studies at Trent. You will build a career, then change that career and change it again as you reinvent your knowledge base multiple times throughout your life.

You will fail as I have many times, including recently when my amazing book proposal was unceremoniously rejected. You will wonder if you're up to the task, as I did trying to crack through the meaning of the blockchain.

At times, you will wonder why the world is not beating a path to your door. Many of you who never dreamed of being entrepreneurs will find yourselves creating a startup. And that's good because new companies are where jobs will come from. You will face adversity.

But it's not what has happened to you that matters, it is how you respond. Recalibrate like I did. Confused? Dig deep and then deeper and you'll figure it out. Reach out to new collaborators and partners to succeed as I did. Build your resilience. Innovate and work harder, and then harder, again.

Play the song "Tubthumping" by Chumbawamba. It has the memorable lyric "I get knocked down, but I get up again." I think there was something in there about a whisky drink and a lager drink, too. Not that your chancellor is advocating the over-consumption of alcohol.

In the face of setback and even defeat, you can choose victory.

Some of you have jobs to go to now. Some not. For those in category number two, view this as a great asset, a time for you to explore, learn, and discover opportunities you didn't know exist.

Your Trent degree will serve you well. As you know, Trent distinguishes itself through its focus on collaborative learning, where students not only receive information but work together to create and test new concepts. Concepts like the fine art of essay or lab procrastination, or how many weeks can a person reasonably avoid doing laundry before someone calls the cops!

Seriously, you all have developed marketable skills, but what really matters in a knowledge economy and a world of collaboration and lifelong learning is your capabilities—your ability to think critically, solve problems, see the big picture, and innovate—and your passion for learning.

Trent describes itself as the champion of collaborative learning that is personal, purposeful, and transformative.

Many of you came to Trent because you care and want to make a difference, not just in your profession but also in the world. And this is a time of great transformation. My hope is that you will be not only effective professionals but agents for change in these troubled times.

I'm sure it's no revelation to you that our society has many problems. Prosperity is on the decline. Leaders of institutions everywhere have lost trust. The global economy is stalled and the world is deeply divided, too unequal, unstable, and unsustainable.

Your generation will need to turn this situation around. Now, I don't mean to put too much pressure on you guys, but I'm kind of pinning all my hopes on you. You'll need to find new solutions as we enter this second generation of the Internet—and each of you will have a role to play.

I'm not suggesting that each of you becomes a candidate for prime minister or world leader. Change will happen in every home, community, business, hospital, clinic, organization, and every nook and cranny of society. It's an opportunity for each of you, if you embrace it. You will need to participate in change in your workplace, community, country, causes you join, and as a global citizen. And you will need to teach your children well.

Your time has come. Now is the time when the world looks to you for hope and inspiration. Now is the time for you to make the changes you want to see in the world. Now is your time.

# CONVOCATION ADDRESS

## Be a Political Person

*Mr. President, graduates, friends, and family:*

Heartfelt congratulations to each of you graduating today and to those who are sharing your success.

Often speeches like this are designed to pass on helpful career advice. But I'm not going to do that, as the data shows you will all have successful careers. You have all chosen fields that make you eminently employable. And your Trent experience has helped to build your capability—for thinking critically, solving problems, understanding context, collaborating, researching, and most important: learning lifelong.

Rather, I want to talk to each of you about your role as a citizen. Let me try to convince you that you should each become a "political" person. Given the low esteem with which people everywhere hold politics, and politicians in particular, you may find this a little odd. But please hear me out.

There are opportunities for you galore, and things are pretty darn good in Canada right now. But overall the world is loaded with problems. We see wealth creation but declining prosperity for most people. There is growing social and economic inequality.

Our planet is unsustainable due to climate change and other factors. The world is conflicted too. National and religious clashes are on the rise. There are more than 100 million refugees and growing. International tensions between nation-states. And once again the threat of nuclear war is raising its ugly head. Recently, in many countries, most notably the United States, we've seen the rise of xenophobia, racism, and the other pernicious trends. Women and gays risk losing many hard-fought rights. The president himself issued an executive order to ban people from entering the United States on the basis of religion.

Everyone is angry.

Now at this point you may be saying, "What a downer! Couldn't we have got the convocation where Mark Zuckerberg is speaking?"

Mark was busy today. So you have me.

And I want to ask each of you what kind of citizen are you going to be.

What will you do to help solve these problems?

In addition to having successful careers, happy families, good friends, and a fulfilling, healthy life, I would like you to consider doing three things:

## 1. Be an informed citizen.

When I graduated from Trent, we got our news from a handful of newspapers and a couple of TV networks. Reporting was generally fair and balanced. Every major publication had an army of fact checkers. There were trusted sources of news such as David Brinkley in the United States. He and his colleagues presented a balanced and considered point of view.

Twenty-five years ago, I wrote a book called the *Digital Economy*. In it I argued that the Internet was a powerful new medium for dissemination of the truth. Indeed, it brought us new ways to distribute

scientific journals, new access to research data, and great informa-
tion sources like Wikipedia. But the dangerous reality is that many
people live in little digital bubbles. They hear only information that
reinforces their beliefs and gives them comfort.

So President Donald Trump bypasses the mainstream media
and tweets that President Barack Obama wiretapped his phones.
Presidents don't have power to wiretap and every law enforcement
agency said the claim was false. Yet according to surveys, close to 40
per cent of the population believes this actually happened.

So I ask you: How are you going to inform yourself in a world
where the old ways of doing that are collapsing?

Some suggestions. Once when I was researching your generation, a
young woman said to me, "If the news is important it will find me."
I thought that was pretty cool at the time, but reflecting on it I've
changed my mind. It's your responsibility to find the news and what's
important. Read the newspaper (online or otherwise). Read whole
articles—including long articles. Listen to CBC (what's left of it).
Develop your BS detectors because there is a lot of BS out there today.

As a society we need to nurture quality journalism, with good judg-
ment, investigative reporting, and balance. I encourage you to stay as
informed as a citizen as you will stay informed of your profession.

## 2. Continue to develop your own view on the world. And be prepared to deepen or change it based on real information and valid data.

What do you think about what's happening in the world?

An example: The United States is the world's most powerful country
and our closest neighbour. Everything it does affects us.

America today is divided. Forty per cent of Americans think President Trump is a great leader who shoots (and tweets) from the hip. They believe he is shaking up the Washington establishment, battling bureaucracy, putting the legitimate rights of Americans first, and getting the country back to work.

But many more think President Trump is a danger to the world, is bereft of morals, and has problems telling the truth. He makes capricious decisions and blames minorities like immigrants for America's problems. He has set out to dismantle health care and the social safety net in the United States so he can reduce taxes for the rich. He doesn't read and is ignorant about world events. He doesn't understand who are democracy's allies (Europe) and its opponents (Russia).

What do you think? Your POV really matters. Let me explain why. President Trump said the mainstream media like the *New York Times* and CNN create fake news in order to discredit him. He said he is the most victimized leader in political history.

But a free and independent media is one of the foundations of a free society. If the media is doing what Trump says, we can't function as a modern democracy.

If Trump is making this up, he is using his office to silence criticism and undermine our basic freedoms.

I do not believe the *New York Times* is fabricating stories. Rather, it is President Trump who is telling lies. I've written for the *New York Times* and their fact checking is relentless. They scrutinized every sentence and demanded I provide evidence for what I was saying. To me the mainstream media is one of the strongest defences against an authoritarian leader.

What do you think?

What do you think about climate change? President Trump has just withdrawn from the Paris agreements. He said climate change is a hoax, perpetuated by the Chinese. But scientists say that climate change is a massive and growing problem. If we reduce carbon emissions 80 per cent by 2050 (a momentous challenge) it will still take 1,000 years for our planet to cool down. And in the meantime bad things will happen. Expect a couple of billion people to lose most of their water supply. We will see the mass displacement of humans and a rise in conflict and death.

What is your view?

Trump wants to renegotiate NAFTA. This will affect all of us. What is your view?

Why is the world so conflicted? Why is there a refugee crisis with tens of millions of displaced refugees? What are the causes of terrorism? How can we stop it? Are you aware of the dangers of growing social inequality? What steps should society take to solve this problem? Is the solution to cut taxes?

How might we solve the problems facing Indigenous peoples? Canada has treated our Indigenous peoples terribly. They continue to face systemic racism and economic subjugation. The Truth and Reconciliation Commission has documented the long history of abuse. Trent has been an international leader on these issues. You may have some important experiences that could help.

A point of view can be a very personal thing, too. For example, what is your "spec" for a partner? Sure, good looks, good fun, and good abs count—but in the long run, common values matter more. If you have children, how will you teach them right from wrong? How will they develop values and want to do the right thing?

How about your community? What are the organizations that make it vibrant, safe, and clean? How could you participate?

## 3. Take a stand. Take action. Become an activist.

I'm not suggesting all of you must take to the streets, run for office, create a blog, or start writing opinion pieces for newspapers.

But rather, the world will only get better if you are involved. I'm talking about you. Not the person next to you. Not your parents or friends. You!

Activism matters. A big reason President Trump was elected was the low voter turnout of young people. I find this heartbreaking. So I encourage you to make a solemn pledge to vote in every federal, provincial, and municipal election for the rest of your life. It is unconscionable to be a citizen in a democratic society and not vote.

Consider joining a community organization or political party. Campaign for ideas you believe in. And if a friend makes a racist, sexist, or homophobic joke, don't let it slide by. Challenge them.

When I left Trent University in 1970, the war in Vietnam was raging. I felt it was an immoral war and that the Vietnamese should determine their own fate. So among other things, I joined the anti-war movement.

This year, more than 45 years later, my wife and I visited Vietnam for the first time. We went into the tunnels where villagers and Vietcong fighters went to escape the bombing. We saw the areas that have been devastated by Agent Orange, from which there are still millions of casualties.

We talked to many people who experienced the war. They told us that they forgive America, as one said, "not for them but for us." They were doing their best to grow a healthy economy. When I mentioned that I had been involved in the antiwar movement, every one of them told us that this movement had made all the difference for them. It changed world opinion and forced the United States to withdraw its troops.

I tell you the story to make a point. You can make a difference.

So please do three things. 1. Be an informed citizen. 2. Have a point of view. 3. And do something.

Be a political person in the best sense of the word, and maybe this smaller world that your children inherit will be a better one. Canada can make a big difference in the world. People increasingly look to us. This is our time and this is your time.

Change will happen and a better world can be forged by you—in every home, community, business, laboratory, organization, and every nook and cranny of society. You will need to participate in change in your workplace, community, country, causes you join, and as a global citizen. And you will need to teach your children well.

Don't take for granted our fragile freedoms and rights. They need to be protected, nurtured, and advanced. We mustn't let the frightening political developments of the United States infect our country. If it can happen in the United States, it can happen anywhere.

I'm enormously confident you can do this because I've studied your generation (and written a couple of books about you). You have the values, the smarts, and will to forge a new future for this little planet and for all of us.

The hopes of the world rest with you. Carry this mantle well. And don't show up at a job interview with your parents.

**2018**

# CONVOCATION ADDRESS

## Thirty-six years from now, how will the world have changed? And what will you have done with your life?

*Mr. President, Mr. Chairman of the Board, graduates, friends, and family:*

Heartfelt congratulations to each of you graduating today and to those who share your success.

You'd never guess this judging from my youthful appearance that I graduated from Trent, almost five decades ago, and reflecting on how the world has changed has caused me to think about the next five decades for you.

In 1970 the war in Vietnam was raging and the Cold War was at its height. The world was divided between communism and capitalism as economic systems. Blacks, women, and Indigenous peoples lacked many basic rights, and almost half of the world's population lived in extreme poverty.

Things have changed a lot, although there is so much to be done. But to me the biggest changes were caused by the advent of the digital age.

Other than TVs, cars, and phones, there was no technology in our lives—and none of that was digital. Nobody used computers except programmers; there were no computers at Trent—anywhere. Our tuition payments were calculated using adding machines and calculators. For my honours thesis, I figured it would take me a year to analyze all the data so I found a ticker tape connection to the one computer in Peterborough at the General Electric plant and programmed some statistical routines. It took fewer than 90 seconds to analyze all my data and I remember thinking, "These computer things are going to be big." I'm not telling you this as some kind of grandpa's fond memories of the good old days. *Au contraire.* Rather I want you to think about how the world is changing and what that might mean for you.

Digital really began to kick in in 1982—the year the IBM personal computer was introduced. Coincidentally that was the year of my first book.

Flash-forward 36 years to today—where technology permeates just about everything. We have AI and machine learning where computers do things they weren't programmed to do because they can learn. Autonomous vehicles are driving on our streets. There are factories full of robots rather than people and drones are delivering parcels. Most important is blockchain—the underlying technology of crypto currencies is challenging the existence of banks, upending many other industries, including government.

The impact has not all been positive. Entire industries have been wiped out. Our privacy has been undermined. Big companies have captured our data—the new oil—and the benefits of digital have been asymmetrical, with growing economies and declining prosperity. There has been a fragmentation of public discourse where we all follow our own point of view in our own little self-reinforcing echo chambers. I'm sure you've all been at a restaurant where people at the table next to you are clicking on their devices and ignoring the people they are with. And drones are not always used for good. But the changes in the last 36 years will pale compared to the changes that you will witness and create. The reason is that growth is exponential, and that digital is moving onto "the second half of the chessboard"—a clever phrase coined by the American inventor and author Ray Kurzweil. He tells a story of the emperor of China being so delighted with the game of chess that he offered the game's inventor any reward he desired. The inventor asked for rice.

"I would like one grain of rice on the first square of the chessboard, two grains of rice on the second square, four grains of rice on the third square, and so on, all the way to the last square," he said. Thinking this would add up to a couple of bags of rice, the emperor happily agreed.

He wasn't very good at math. While small at the outset, the amount of rice escalates to more than 2 billion grains halfway (36 squares) through the chessboard. The final square would require two to the 64th—18 quintillion, 464 quadrillion, 744 trillion grains of rice— enough to cover all of Earth.

So imagine the effect of this exponential growth as in this year— 2018—we enter the second half. The last 36 years will look like a little quaint blip compared to the massive changes that are coming—and doubling next year and doubling after that and so on. Think about technology quintillions of times more capable than that measly dumb thing in our pockets today or in the Trent data centre.

The implications for you are profound but they don't have to be staggering. And the good news is that your Trent education has equipped you well to survive on this second half of the chess board.

Some advice. Design your life. Don't let the future just happen. Achieve a future that works for you, your family, your community, and the world.

## 1. Design your strategy for lifelong learning

My colleagues and I entered the workforce with a base of knowledge and "kept up" in our chosen field. We thought we were set for life. Today you know this idea is laughable. If your degree only marked a milestone in your knowledge, you'd be set for (to use Andy Warhol's aphorism) about 15 minutes. Much of what you learned in your first year is obsolete. I know you're celebrating a milestone today, but don't think that your higher education is completed. It has just begun.

Lifelong learning is an assumption for you; you'll need to reinvent your knowledge base multiple times as you go through life. And as graduates from a liberal arts and sciences university, you know that it's not just your knowledge that's important. It's your ability to think, collaborate, solve problems, synthesize, and learn and learn again, again, and again.

Also, I encourage you to plan your media diet. When I graduated, we had a few network TV stations and newspapers that we all relied on and we could trust the news anchors to tell us the truth.

Today you have millions of choices where you get your information. You need to develop your BS detectors and make choices about how you will interact with this avalanche of information. Don't be cynical about what you read and see but be skeptical. The antidote to information overload is to develop your personal filters. And don't just scan—read at least a couple of articles every day from beginning to end.

## 2. Design your vocation

When I graduated from Trent, students wanted to work for a big company like IBM, GM, a consulting company, a big bank or get a job as a teacher or government employee. Today these options are less feasible as hiring has declined. However, there are new choices and a big one is to be an entrepreneur.

Research shows that most new jobs come from relatively new companies. Entrepreneurship is the key to jobs. There is a lesson here for you. Look for opportunities to join small companies, not just big organizations. Or do the unthinkable. Explore the idea of creating your own business. Small companies can now have all the capabilities of large companies without all the liabilities—legacy cultures, systems, and processes.

This doesn't mean throw caution to the wind and get your parents to mortgage their house to fund your big idea. Typically, it makes sense to get some work experience and to develop an idea, business plan, and the connections to make it happen. But you might be one of the new generation of business builders who will make a real difference in achieving prosperity in Canada. Or by being a social entrepreneur you can do well by doing good in the world at the same time. Which brings me to my final point.

## 3. Design your life as a citizen

Today your degree from Trent equips you well for thinking, collaborating, researching, solving problems and lifelong learning. So, as you leave these hallowed halls by all means (as Spock would say) "Live long and prosper." Build a successful and prosperous life for yourselves and your families.

But let me argue that humanity needs more of you. As you travel through this second half of the chessboard, I don't think it's an exaggeration to say that pretty much everything we know about civilization will change. Most industries, companies, and job types will not exist at the end of the board. You will be the generation to lead in rebuilding our institutions, economy, and society.

So my hope is that you will each design your life to be a consequential one—beyond your vocation.

You will need to participate in change in your workplace, community, country, causes you join, and as a global citizen. And you will need to teach your children well.

One simple thing you can do is to just vote! All around the world young people are cynical about our political institutions. But don't give up on democracy. The alternatives for you, your future families, and loved ones are not desirable. So I encourage you to be a political person—with a small P—for starters by voting in every election that comes along.

I say this on an auspicious occasion—not just your graduation but today is an election day in Ontario. You can make it a perfect day by voting.

Canada needs your good judgment, critical thinking, passion, and demographic muscle to ensure that this smaller country your children inherit is a better one.

I have never been more optimistic about the future because I believe we are in the early days of a new civilization—one that is enabled by a communications revolution and forged by young people around the world. Because each of you can participate in this new renaissance, it is surely an amazing time to graduate and to be alive.

I hope you will have the wisdom and the will to seize the time and design your life to make it work for you and for our collective future.

# ADDRESS TO FACULTY AND STUDENTS

## Toward a New Social Contract for the Digital Economy

Will this smaller world your children inherit be a better one? And what is to be done to ensure that it is? Let me tell you a humbling story. Writing the 20th-anniversary edition of my 1994 book *The Digital Economy* was a sobering experience. The book was very positive about the "promise of the Internet" and to be sure the Net has brought about many great innovations.

But the book has a small section about the Dark Side—things that could go wrong. Re-reading it 20 years later, I was shocked to see that every danger I hypothesized has materialized. Our privacy has been undermined. The digital economy has created a system of "digital feudalism," wherein a tiny few have appropriated the largesse of this new era of prosperity. Data, the oil of the 21st century, is not owned by those who create it. Rather, it's controlled by an increasingly centralized group of "digital landlords," who collect, aggregate, and profit from the data that collectively constitutes our digital identities. Exploiting our data has enabled them to achieve unprecedented wealth, while at the same time the middle class and prosperity are stalled.

In 1994 I hoped the Internet would create new industries and jobs and it did for a while. But today technology is wiping out entire industries; underemployment and the threat of structural employment are fuelling unrest. Trucking, one of Canada's largest sources of employment, will likely be automated within a decade. Digitized networks enable outsourcing, offshoring, and the globalization of labour. Within the second era of the digital age—one centred on blockchain technologies, machine learning, artificial intelligence, robotics, and the Internet of Things—many core functions of knowledge work, many companies and industries are in jeopardy.

Yes, there is a new wave of entrepreneurism globally, but our regulations were designed for the old industrial economy and hamper success.

The increased transparency enabled by the Internet has also revealed deep problems in society. Canada is learning the truth about the horrific history of our Indigenous peoples, who in turn now have tools to speak out and organize collective action. We also understand deeply how climate change threatens civilization on this planet and people, especially young people who will suffer most and who are now organizing to re-industrialize the country and the world.

I had hoped the Internet would bring us together as societies and improve our democracies. But the opposite has occurred. We are often exposed solely to information and perspectives that reinforce our own views, with information and perspectives filtered to accommodate our pre-existing biases. The upshot has been more fracturing and divisive public discourse; democratic institutions are eroding before our eyes, as trust in politicians and the legitimacy of our governments is at an all-time low.

Populist rhetoric becomes more appealing in these conditions, and many are vulnerable to scapegoating and xenophobia. The upshot is there is a crisis of legitimacy of liberal democracy.

To misquote the 1976 film *Network*: "People everywhere are mad as hell and they're not going to take it anymore."

Perhaps as unthinkable as the success of Donald Trump is the rise of Bernie Sanders, an avowed socialist who has almost won the democratic presidential nomination. The unfolding story is one of growing discontent with the deepening economic crisis and the old establishment that created it.

All this came together recently with Brexit, then Donald Trump—a kind of one-two punch, smacking the world in the face. Centrist parties are in rapid decline and extremist right-wing parties from Hungary and Poland to France and Germany are on the rise. In other countries, particularly in southern Europe where memories of dictatorship and fascism are still raw, the left is ascendant.

The world has seen this story before, in the lead-up to the Second World War, but the analogy is imperfect. Among other things, the rate of change is different. As the digital revolution unfolds, it is driving profound changes in the global economy, labour markets, old institutions, and society as a whole. It is enabling spectacular innovation and unprecedented wealth creation. At the same time, growing social inequality, the decline of the middle class, pernicious unemployment, and underemployment are fuelling unrest. Networks enable outsourcing, offshoring, and the globalization of labour markets. Government architectures and policies have not evolved, and there is a fiscal crisis and threat to the industrial-age social safety net everywhere.

Data, a new asset class, has been captured by powerful forces, and one result is the continual erosion of personal privacy and prosperity as a small handful of companies captures the largesse of the digital age asymmetrically. Climate change is threatening our biosphere with huge displacement and other disruptions just beginning to be felt. Meanwhile industrial-age institutions for solving global problems—based on the Bretton Woods model of global institutions—are stalled. The upshot is that the social contract—the agreements, laws, and appropriate behaviours people, companies, civil society, and their governments abide by—no longer serves us well.

Conversely, the next era of the digital economy could bring a new epoch of prosperity, with new networked models of global problem solving to realize such a dream. The reason is that we're entering a second era of the digital age. For the last 40 years we've seen the rise of mainframes, minicomputers, the PC, the Internet, mobility, the web, the mobile web, social media, the cloud, and big data. We're entering a second era where new technologies are being infused into everything and every business process. Innovations such as artificial intelligence (AI), machine learning, the Internet of Things (IoT), robotics, even technology in our bodies, drones, robots, and new materials are enabling entirely new types of enterprises. Foundational to these innovations is the underlying technology of crypto currencies: blockchain.

To meet these new challenges, the time has come for governments everywhere to provide leadership in reimagining our social contracts—the basic expectations between business, government, and civil society—and to redo their budgets, putting their money behind some fresh new thinking. When we evolved from an agrarian economy to an industrial one, we developed a new social contract for the times—public education, a social safety net, and laws about civil rights, pollution, workplace safety, and financial markets, to name a few. Countless nongovernmental civil society organizations arose to help solve problems. It is time to update these agreements, create new institutions, and renew the expectations and responsibilities that citizens should have about society.

We need new networked models of global problem solving. The next era of the digital economy could bring a new epoch of prosperity, if we rely on multi-stakeholder approaches to effect change. By that, I mean groups of independent parties who organize around the big problems we need to solve—not just health, education, and justice but social safety and environmental stability—the right to clean air, safe water, sustainable food sources, and ecologically sound homelands in perpetuity. People from government, the private sector, and civil society could forge and agree on new action plans and budgets.

We need new models for citizen engagement. Networks enable citizens to participate fully in their own governance, and we can now move to a second era of democracy based on a culture of public deliberation and active citizenship. Mandatory voting encourages active, engaged, and responsible citizens, but only if voters can cast their ballots easily, securely, and without intimidation. Technologies such as blockchain, for example, enable us to embed electoral promises into smart contracts and to secure other forms of direct democracy through the mobile platforms citizens use every day.

We need new models of work and education. Our expectations of employment are shifting. People no longer anticipate doing the same job in the same company in the same field their whole career. To support transitions, we need a universal basic income that supports entrepreneurialism and investing in the potential of individuals. Students today are preparing for unprecedented lifelong learning, with the knowledge that technology will likely force them to reimagine their role in the workforce. We need to transform how we educate young people in all zip codes for this future.

We need new models of identity. Let's move away from the industrial-age system of stamps, seals, and signatures we depend on to this day. We need to protect the security of personhood and end the systems of economic exclusion, digital feudalism, and migrant deportation. Individuals should own and profit from the data they create from the moment of their birth. These are just some of the dimensions of a new contract. Call it a Declaration of Interdependence for the Digital Age.[1]

It's also time for business executives to participate responsibly—for their own long-term survival and the health of the economy and the planet overall. Even—or especially—in a time of exploding information online, we need scientists, researchers, and journalists to seek the truth, examine options, and inform the ongoing public conversation.

Are these expectations overly utopian? Only if we don't put money behind them. These efforts require serious overhaul of government budgets, a reallocation of public resources, where we invest in every person's success rather than profiteer from their failure. We anticipate a real crisis of leadership because the status quo is indefensible to anyone with a conscience. It is my hope that these dark and painful days call forth a new generation of leaders who can help us bring everyone into the digital age. Who among us will step up?

# Note

1.  The Declaration of Interdependence, by Don Tapscott. 2018.
    https://dontapscott.com/research-programs/social-contract

# CONVOCATION ADDRESS

## Some unconventional advice for business graduates

*Mr. President, Mr. Chairman of the Board, graduates, friends, and family:*

Heartfelt congratulations to each of you graduating today and to those who share your success. I must tell you that the last six years of being your chancellor have been one of the greatest honours and most rewarding experiences of my life. So, to all of you in the Trent community, thank you.

I'd like to take this opportunity to share some unconventional advice, drawing from the experience of my own life as a Trent graduate.

In the late 1970s, I was hired as a researcher at Canada's Bell Labs (Bell Northern Research) in Toronto. I knew hardly anything about technology, but I got the job because I had expertise, learned in the psych department at Trent and later University of Alberta about research methodology. Our group was trying to figure out how "internetworked computers" used by professionals and managers could change "knowledge work" and the nature of organizations.

Our group conducted the first-ever controlled experiments about the impact of technology on knowledge work. Half the office worked the old way—with telephones, typing pools, manual calendars, filing cabinets, and the corporate library for information. The other half had computers on their desks connected to digital networks. They used a suite of tools that we built for electronic mail, word processing, document co-authoring and management, online information retrieval, personal time management and calendaring, and financial planning tools (spreadsheets had not been invented yet).

We found that the wired group performed better and had more fun, concluding that computers were going to go beyond data processing to be used by everyone as communications tools. I was very fortunate to end up there, as we were doing work 15 years ahead of its time. In our group were people who today I still remember fondly as brilliant.

I wrote a book about that experience in 1981, but it didn't sell well. Critics said only programmers would use computers because regular people would never learn to type.

Regardless, I was on the executive fast track. I had received four promotions in two years and was running the entire division of the company from my massive corner office. Even though our ideas didn't yet have broad acceptance, I was a rising star in the company and highly regarded as a digital pioneer among the global "digerati" of the time.

Which is why it seemed so weird when a colleague named Del Langdon tried to convince me to quit the company and become an entrepreneur. It was circa 1982, in the middle of a brutal recession, and I was about to launch a family. And here I had this colleague argue that we should take a dozen people in our division and create a company to help people implement this new class of technology— even though the technology didn't exist. In fact, when we left the company, the IBM PC had not yet appeared on the market; it would be a full decade before PCs communicated with other technologies in a reasonable manner.

Her advice seemed nuts, but something caused me to listen. With the advantage of hindsight I can reflect on my reasons, unarticulated at the time: we wanted to control our own destiny; we wanted to share in the wealth we created; but most of all, I think we wanted the freedom to try to change the world—to create technology that would transform the way people worked, learned and communicated.

We were partially successful. We consulted for companies and governments, leading some of the earliest implementations of networked workstations in the world. We wrote a book together, which had a modest impact. We built a system that eventually was acquired. The IPO didn't exactly bring us great wealth, but it led to more good things. Eventually, we lost control of the company. That chapter ended unhappily.

But the legacy was a great one—including that our colleagues all went on to do very interesting work. As for me, I finally wrote a book that someone read—*Paradigm Shift*, in 1992—as I started to get that market timing thing down better. This led to a string of bestsellers: *The Digital Economy*, *Growing Up Digital*, *Wikinomics*, and a dozen others, most recently with my son, Alex, *Blockchain Revolution*. It also led to the creation of companies that were significant both in terms of wealth creation and impact in the world.

Today, I feel very fortunate. I am truly the master of my destiny. I have a prosperous and purposeful life beyond my early dreams and am so fortunate to have a lifelong marriage, two wonderful children, and now three beautiful grandchildren.

So let me share some unconventional wisdom from that experience. Call it "the seven truths that highly successful professionals should upend."

### 1. Don't get a job. Consider starting your own business.

Some work experience in a large organization is valuable. But the turning point in my professional life was when I left the executive track at Bell Northern Research to become an entrepreneur. Today, more and more people will make this choice, leveraging the Internet and emerging technologies like blockchain and artificial intelligence. Many will fail, as I did (several times). But for many more, the experience will be worth it.

### 2. Don't seek work-life balance. Do what you love.

Your day should not divided between work and having a life. Find or make work that is meaningful and enjoyable. And when off work, spend some time doing productive activities. At Bell Northern Research, we looked forward to our work every day. We were passionate about it, and I remain excited by what I'm doing every day. During a one-day session with the management of a Fortune 20 company, I brought in a panel of new employees. One executive asked them, "What could we do to make our company more attractive to your generation?" Without missing a beat, one new employee said, "Make this place more fun. It's just not fun to work here." By fun, she meant collaborative, integrated with learning, solving meaningful problems. You can be the generation to transform the nature of work, so that's part of life.

### 3. Don't be a good manager. Be a great leader.

You've all studied the discipline of management. As Peter Drucker said years ago, stable times require excellence and good managers. As we transition to a new age, our organizations need more than management; they need leadership. Rather than manage the status quo, lead the change. Think of yourself primarily as a leader as we did at Bell Northern Research. These times don't require organizational tinkering; they require deep innovation and transformation.

## 4. Don't ever graduate. Be a lifelong learner.

Parents, don't freak out on me here. I'm just suggesting to your children that they take the time to develop a strategy for lifelong learning and to be an informed citizen—for life. Develop a strategy for learning as an innovator, a leader, a professor, a parent, and a citizen. Society needs informed participants. Knowledge is exploding around you, and so you need to commit to reinventing your knowledge base multiple times throughout your lifetime. Consider getting a graduate degree because a BA today is like a high school education decades ago. As you leave here, remember, it's not only what you know that counts—it's also your ability to think critically, research, solve problems, and collaborate on solutions that matters.

## 5. Don't seek happiness. Live a purposeful life.

This is a tough one. We all want to be happy, but in my experience, happiness has been a by-product of living a purposeful life, rich with meaningful relationships. In the decades ahead, you will see staggering changes in the world. You will be more fulfilled if you participate fully in these transformations rather than stand on the sidelines. Build a deep network of loved ones, and happiness will be the result.

## 6. Don't wish for luck. Be ready for your big break.

For me, good fortune has always come at the intersection of preparation and opportunity. My university degrees prepared me, and I was open to opportunity when it came knocking. You are similarly prepared, and I have no doubt that each of you will fund your own path to prosperity. What an amazing time to graduate! Business is undergoing great transformation, and as many opportunities await you as you can create for yourselves.

## 7. Don't build shareholder value. Cultivate all stakeholders.

The best way to create value for shareholders is to build it for customers, employees, and the communities in which your business operates. As you enter the workforce, you will have the best tools for innovating, engaging all stakeholders and building new businesses. So think about everyone that matters, not just business owners. True even if *you* are the owner of the business.

The data shows that you will all be successful and your Trent degree has equipped you for that.

So as you leave this wonderful institution, by all means "live long and prosper" (as Spock would say). Build a prosperous life for yourselves and your families. But let me conclude that humanity needs more of you.

The world you are entering is full of opportunity but as a business person and as a citizen, you will face growing challenges, such as the crises of climate change and the declining legitimacy of democracy. Trade wars are looming. Leaders of institutions everywhere have lost the public trust. Massive corporations are capturing our data and undermining our privacy while they enrich themselves. We need to recover our digital identities so that we can manage all this data to serve ourselves, not just them. For the first time in modern history our economies are growing but prosperity for most is stalled or declining. The global economy is unstable, and the world is deeply divided.

I believe that business can't succeed in a world that's failing.

Your generation is being called on to ensure that the smaller world your children inherit is a prosperous, just, and sustainable one.

You can participate in changing your workplace, your community, and your country as a global citizen. You must teach your children well. And you must exercise your right to vote—something precious and rare in the world today.

Wherever you are, design your life. Live the values of your generation. Continue your university experience with a full life that is purposeful, transformational, and consequential.

So again, congratulations to all of you. Think beyond the traditional paradigm and assumptions of business today. Dream big. Make a difference. As Dr. Michael Cooke said to the convocating class yesterday—don't just make a living, make your mark.

My hope for you is that each of you will live a principled life of consequence.

# CHANCELLOR RETIREMENT SPEECH

## Dinner celebrating
## Dr. Don Tapscott '66 as
## Trent University's 11th Chancellor

I was the first of four Tapscott boys to attend Trent University. Miraculously, we all graduated too. Standing here in the magnificent Ron Thom Great Hall, I'm flooded with memories. The late 1960s was an amazing time to be a student. The world was opening up and changing. Everything was possible. I remember standing on this stage giving a speech about the war in Vietnam and mobilizing students to protest. Trent became a leader in the antiwar movement taking caravans of buses to Toronto to attend the big protests of the early 70s.

Just around the corner is a room that the university let me and my band use to practise. We set up our equipment there and it was our room. I remember the amazing head of the psychology department, Alan Worthington, who taught me to be a good researcher and the brilliant (and I can think of half a dozen people I've met since then for whom I would use that adjective) sociology professor Pradeep Bandyopadhyay who introduced me to Karl Marx. It turns out that

(L to R) Mary Tapscott, Dr. Don Tapscott, CM, and his wife Ana Lopes, CM, on the occasion of Don's installation as Trent University's first alumnus Chancellor on June 7, 2013. During this ceremony, the academic regalia is removed and the Chancellor regalia (the gown and hat seen here) are bestowed upon the Chancellor.

(L to R) Professor David Newhouse, Dr. Robin Quantick, Chancellor Don Tapscott, Dr. Mark Angelo, and President Leo Groarke on June 4, 2019. Chancellor Don Tapscott conferred an honorary degree on Dr. Mark Angelo during convocation in recognition of his work in the area of river conservation in Canada and throughout the world. *Photo courtesy of Trent University.*

Ad printed in the *Globe and Mail* the first week of June 2019, celebrating the Chancellor transition as Don Tapscott concluded his term and Stephen Stohn was installed as Trent's next Chancellor. Digital guru Don Tapscott and entertainment powerhouse Stephen Stohn credit Trent University's "secret sauce" with providing an incomparable foundation for their success. Trent's first alumnus Chancellor, Don, passed the torch to Trent's second alumnus Chancellor, Stephen. It was an historic moment for the University and for these good friends from the class of '66. *Poster courtesy of Trent University.*

Event poster for the Chancellor Lecture Series: New Ideas for a Connected Planet. During this lecture series, Chancellor Don Tapscott delivered three speeches in Southern Ontario: "Solving Global Problems Differently" in Peterborough, "Creating 21st Century Cities" in Oshawa, and "Government & Democracy in the Networked Age" in Toronto. *Poster courtesy of Trent University.*

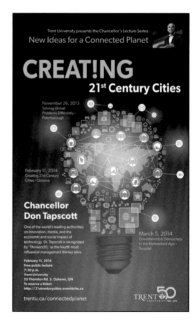

(L to R) Professor David Newhouse, Board Chair Stephen Kylie, President and Vice-Chancellor Leo Groarke, Dr. Asaf Zohar, honorary degree recipient Dr. George Cope, and Chancellor Don Tapscott on June 5, 2018. Dr. Cope, President and CEO of BCE Inc. and Bell Canada, was the recipient of an honorary degree during convocation in recognition of his outstanding work as a corporate leader and champion for mental health. *Photo courtesy of Trent University.*

Chancellor Don Tapscott celebrates with a new Trent University Bachelor of Arts graduate and his family after the convocation ceremony. *Photo courtesy of Trent University.*

Chancellor Don Tapscott during a tour of a science lab at Trent University. *Photo courtesy of Trent University.*

Chancellor Don Tapscott takes a selfie with graduating students during a convocation ceremony. The Chancellor selfie became a tradition of Chancellor Tapscott's other convocations and with students and their families after each ceremony he presided over.

Chancellor Don Tapscott and a group of nursing students after their convocation ceremony. *Photo courtesy of Trent University.*

Chancellor Tapscott speaks to an audience of tens of thousands of people at the Helsinki Business Forum in 2017. *Photo courtesy of Helsinki Business Forum.*

Chancellor Don Tapscott speaks in Shanghai for the Chinese technology company Tencent. *Photo courtesy of Tencent.*

Chancellor Don Tapscott guest-edits the *Toronto Star* (Canada's largest circulation newspaper) May 7, 2016. He wrote or curated dozens of articles around the theme of "innovation," exploring how Canada could lead the world in a time of transformation, and showcased groundbreaking thinking, research and development, and policy making across all sectors. *Poster courtesy of the Toronto Star.*

the world has changed a lot since Marx, but even today a lot of what he had to say about capitalism is profound. And of course there was the omnipresent Tom Symons, Trent's founding president, who got to know me from the first day I was there and has keep in touch to this day.

## A Joy Being Chancellor

Being chancellor has been one of the greatest professional joys of my life. I suppose on the continuum of active versus purely ceremonial chancellors, I have been fairly active. It's been great being on campus, giving presentations, in various cities in different countries, helping to raise funds, participating in the media and public dialogue on behalf of Trent, and getting to meet and work with dozens of amazing people on campus. For sure I've made some dear friends!

Probably the greatest joy has been meeting the students, including at convocations. Watching those bright eyes and happy faces come across the stage is inspiring—every one of them.

Sometimes it becomes very personal. One example was a Muslim woman wearing a hijab who approached me and asked, "Is it okay if I don't shake your hand?" I said of course and began to talk to her about what she had studied. We turned to the photographer for the official photo and I wished her well, of course respecting that her religious beliefs precluded me from touching her in any way. Afterwards she came up to me with a rose that had been given to her and she asked that I keep it. She told me that she had been worried this would be the most embarrassing day of her life because unlike other students, she would not be able to shake my hand in front of the audience—but that it had ended up being an effortless and beautiful moment on stage.

My first experience as chancellor produced a kind of humbling story. When I agreed to be chancellor, I went to a special building in Toronto where they make gowns and other ceremonial clothing for officials like judges and academics. I told the manager there, half joking, that I wanted to reinvent the chancellor gown, perhaps with a trim euro cut, a big fur collar, maybe ermine, and a lot of colours. He told me that this was simply not possible and that tradition dictated I wear the official Trent Chancellor Gown, sized to me—a specialized discreet dark green gown covered in beautiful gold embroidery. He told me that the embroidery alone took a craftsperson three months to complete. Thinking about it, this seemed really sweet, but I asked him if at least there were any customizations possible. He got a devilish look in his eye and whispered to me that we could make it longer than the standard cut of eight inches from the ground. I asked him if that would be revolutionary and he enthusiastically agreed that it would be. So I'm proud to say that my first act as chancellor was one of rebellion, and my gown reaches down to four inches above the ground! (Since I graduated from Trent my opinion of what constituted "revolutionary" has certainly evolved.)

I've learned a lot too. Perhaps the greatest area was to understand more deeply the awful history, challenges, and beauty of our Indigenous people. I've always argued for the rights of Indigenous Peoples and redressing the terrible crimes and systemic oppression they have faced. But I've been awakened in my recent years here to the many wondrous and meaningful traditions and teachings of this powerful community at Trent, and I thank the many people I've met.

# Honestly? Mixed Feelings About Giving Up My Chancellor Role

Let me close on a light note, as I confess to having mixed feelings about passing the role, duties, and honour to my good friend Stephen Stohn. I've been a chancellor for two terms and it was my suggestion to President Groarke ("Mr. Vice-Chancellor" as I like to call him) that it was time for a change. But over the past three days I've been feeling a little *verklempt*, grieving a bit—perhaps even going through Elisabeth Kübler-Ross's Five Stages of Grief.

First was Denial. I started thinking if China's president Xi could be president for life, why couldn't I be chancellor for life? Next was Anger. I started grumbling to myself "Who is this Stephen Stohn guy?" Then Bargaining. I thought to myself, "Maybe I could be a shadow chancellor—I could have a weekly lunch with Chancellor Stohn to provide my, um, helpful advice." Then Depression, as the realization of my impending doom set in. Ultimately, however, I came to Acceptance.

Seriously, I'm really good with this and now is the time to move on. Upon reflection, Stephen is a brilliant choice. He is a most accomplished Canadian with great integrity. Oh—and another thing—he is from the class of 1966–1970, clearly supporting the mythology that this is perhaps the, um, greatest class ever.

# Advice to the New Chancellor

This morning an interviewer from the CHEX TV crew asked me to give some advice for the new chancellor. I told them that Stephen hardly needed advice from me, and that I looked forward to seeing how he personalized the role as I had done.

However, in a moment of reflection and sober second thought, I do have some clear and very strong suggestions:

1. **Remember.** A chancellor is like a bidet. No one really knows what it's for, but everyone is pleased to have one. Work with that.

2. **Under your term you can finally resolve The BIG Debate.** When referring to yourself should it be "The Chancellor" or simply "Chancellor." Ana and I were attending a wedding in St. James's Palace—as the butler said, "the senior palace in the UK realm." We were talking to a protocol expert and I mentioned that I was The Chancellor of Trent University. She was horrified, explaining that I was in fact chancellor. Now given the many other burning debates and issues in the world, this may seem relatively trivial to you, but I say to you today that this is a matter of great importance.

3. **My most important advice to you—and I mean this with all seriousness—is to keep an eye on the vice-chancellor, Leo Groarke.** (Like me, I recommend you refer to him as vice-chancellor, not president.) Beware. There have been numerous disturbing developments I've noticed that suggest he is attempting to move in on chancellor powers and responsibilities and possibly become the chancellor himself. This is tantamount to a coup in the making:

   - The vice-chancellor has a gown embroidered in silver. The chancellor's gown is embroidered in gold. However, more than once the vice-chancellor has "mistakenly" donned the chancellor's gown. An accident you say!?

- The chancellor is at the front of the convocation procession but on three occasions this week I found the vice-chancellor "mistakenly" in that spot.

- As chancellor I order a Tall latte—affectionately known as The Chancellor's Latte. The vice-chancellor has now joined in, but get this—he is now ordering a Grande latte. What's next—Venti! This kind of one-upmanship has got to be stopped.

These are all symptoms of an insatiable thirst for power. Grave consequences for the future of Trent and the future of liberal and sciences education. I say to you Stephen, Beware. And fight back.

On a more serious note, one of my greatest delights over the last six years has been to watch and even participate a bit in the "Trent Turnaround." Trent is on a roll, growing, thriving, and ranking spectacularly and superlatively among its peers. More than anything it has to do with the leadership of President Leo Groarke. We've become great friends and it's been a delight to get to know Glennice at our cottage some summers. I have had an effortless collaboration with a wise leader and I'm sure Stephen will too.

Thank you to all of you. Being chancellor of Trent has been an honour. And of course, I will continue to be involved and support Trent in any way that you want.

To my good friend Stephen: you have my great admiration and heartfelt best wishes.

# CONVOCATION DINNER CELEBRATING CHANCELLOR DON TAPSCOTT

## Remarks by Leo Groarke, President and Vice-Chancellor

Chancellor Dr. Don Tapscott, class of '66. Don began his term as chancellor in 2013, and he is the first alumnus to be chancellor at Trent.

Don is one of the world's leading authorities on the impact of technology on business and society. His 1992 bestseller, *Paradigm Shift*, helped coin this seminal management concept, and *The Digital Economy*, written in 1995, changed business thinking about the transformational nature of the Internet. Two years later he helped popularize the terms "Net Generation" and "the Digital Divide" in his book *Growing Up Digital*. In all, he has authored 16 books, including *Wikinomics: How Mass Collaboration Changes Everything*, which has been translated into over 25 languages.

Prior to becoming chancellor, Don served as chair of Trent's Beyond Our Walls fundraising campaign in the mid-1990s, which raised more than $17 million to advance Trent's mission. In 2006 he was awarded an honorary degree by Trent for his accomplishments and service.

Don arrived as our first alum chancellor at a very important time in our evolution as a university—the cusp of our 50th anniversary. And the beginning of my term as president.

Don was able to preside over Trent's 50th anniversary celebrations: as the keynote speaker for the alumni reunion and symposium, speaker at the anniversary gala, and walking in the lead of the community parade along downtown Peterborough.

During his six years as chancellor, Don will have presided over 47 convocation ceremonies, and after his last convocation, Don will have shaken the hands of more than 7,200 students!

Don also spoke to Trent students and the community at multiple venues throughout his term and hosted gatherings of Trent alumni around the world, including New York and London, England.

Don also had the good fortune to attend and help celebrate the grand opening of the Student Centre and transformation of the Bata Library.

Since he assumed his role as chancellor, Don has moved up in the rankings of the Thinkers50 global ranking of management thinkers from ninth, to fourth, and mostly recently to second in 2017; and was recognized as the top Digital Thinker in the world. I'd like to think Trent had something to do with that!

Also, in 2016 Don received the Order of Canada for his leadership in the field of business innovation and the social impact of information technology.

Don's global reputation brought attention to Trent University and he proudly championed Trent wherever he went.

Before and during his tenure, Don, and his wife Ana Lopes, continued to be generous donors to Trent.

Thank you, Don, for all you have done while serving your term as chancellor, and for being a role model to students who seek to live a life of consequence.

# SELECTED ARTICLES ABOUT ISSUES ABOUT ISSUES FACING STUDENTS

# TORONTO STAR

## Business cannot succeed in a world that is failing

DON TAPSCOTT, TORONTO, ON, MAY 2013: B.1

*"Capitalism is the Crisis" (Occupy Wall Street Sign).*

The industrial age is finally coming to an end, and with it the old model of capitalism is ending as well.

The continuing global economic mess, growing inequalities, and environmental destruction, to name a few crises, are causing many to ask: Is global capitalism fixable as a system, and if so, what is to be done?

While free enterprise and markets have proven essential for product innovation, all around us we see industries in crisis and governments that can't get things done. Old media companies are failing, and a few years ago the core modus operandi of Wall Street basically imploded. Schools and universities teach with century-old methods.

Global cooperation and problem-solving institutions such as the World Bank, the UN, and the G20 seem impotent.

Youth unemployment is a global epidemic, and as young people choose increasingly not to vote, democratic institutions face a crisis of legitimacy.

During capitalism's first iteration, the means of production was machinery. The most important assets were physical and financial.

Companies had command-and-control hierarchies, and capitalists focused on maximizing personal wealth.

No longer. The most important assets now are in the crania of knowledge workers, and the most effective work systems are social and collaborative. Citizens increasingly realize that an economy driven solely by greed, with companies interested only in shareholder value, is unworkable and threatens the planet.

We're in the early stages of a massive transformation. Just like the printing press moved the world from a feudal, agrarian society to industrial capitalism, the Internet ushers in a new era.

Close to a billion people use social media daily. In 10 years, the number of Internet users will soar from 2 billion to 7 billion. Today, 80 per cent of the world's population uses cellphones. The social world is transforming the way we create wealth, work, learn, play, raise our children, and probably the way we think.

We're all collaborating like never before, and in business the hottest concepts are social—collective intelligence, mass collaboration, crowdsourcing, and collaborative innovation.

As knowledge becomes more distributed, so does power.

People are becoming smarter, scrutinizing institutions, organizing collectively, and forging innovative ways of doing almost everything. Peers are creating encyclopedias and new ways of funding entrepreneurship. Wikirevolutions are challenging tyrants.

For capitalism to have a future, it must change fundamentally.

We need to understand that business can't succeed in a world that's failing. We need to bake integrity into corporate DNA.

A good start is to rethink executive pay packages so that corporate leaders are motivated to do the right thing.

Industrial capitalism brought representative democracy, but with a weak public mandate and inert citizenry. The digital age offers a new democracy based on public deliberation and active citizenship.

We need collaboration in areas such as education, health care, and science. Cities must become open, with smart power grids, intelligent transportation systems, and transparent government.

Change is required urgently and the contours of a new model are emerging.

But we need leadership to make this transition. Many leaders of industrial capitalism will resist. History tells us those who don't join in will be swept away.

# THE GLOBE AND MAIL

## Economist Ronald Coase's theories predicted the Internet's impact on how business is done

DON TAPSCOTT, TORONTO, ON, 9 SEPTEMBER 2013

## Digital revolution

Renowned economist Ronald Coase died last week at the age of 102. Among his many achievements, Mr. Coase was awarded the 1991 Nobel Prize in economics, largely for his inspiring 1937 paper, "The Nature of the Firm."

Mr. Coase's enduring legacy may well be that 60 years later, his paper and theories help us understand the Internet's impact on business, the economy, and all our institutions.

Back when the Internet was still called the information superhighway, I began forecasting the impact of ubiquitous connectivity. Much of my thinking was shaped by Mr. Coase's early work.

As a young economist, Mr. Coase was perplexed by large American companies run by titans such as Henry Ford and Alfred Sloan Jr. If the free market was the best way to allocate resources, why did these capitalists run their companies in much the same way as Stalin ran the Soviet Union's economy?

The upshot is that most vertically integrated corporations found it cheaper and simpler to perform most functions in-house, rather than incurring the cost, hassle, and risk of constant transactions with outside partners.

It makes sense for a firm to expand until the cost of performing a transaction inside the firm exceeds the cost of performing the transaction outside the firm. This is why large, insular corporations prevailed in the industrial economy.

This is no longer the case. Many behemoths have lost market share to more supple competitors. Digital technologies slash transaction and collaboration costs. Smart companies are making their boundaries porous, using the Internet to harness knowledge, resources, and capabilities outside the company.

Today's economic engines are Internet-based clusters of businesses. While each company retains its identity, companies function together, creating more wealth than they could ever hope to create individually. Where corporations were once gigantic, new business ecosystems tend toward the amorphous.

Procter and Gamble now gets 60 per cent of its innovation from outside corporate walls. Boeing has built a massive ecosystem to design and manufacture jumbo jets. China's motorcycle industry, which consists of dozens of companies collaborating with no single company pulling the strings, now comprises 40 per cent of global motorcycle production.

Looked at one way, Amazon.com is a website with many employees that ships books. Looked at another way, however, Amazon is a vast ecosystem that includes authors, publishers, customers who write reviews for the site, delivery companies like UPS, and tens of thousands of affiliates that market products and arrange fulfillment through the Amazon network. Hundreds of thousands of people are involved in Amazon's viral marketing network.

This is leading to the biggest change to the corporation in a century and altering how we orchestrate capability to innovate, create goods and services, and engage with the world. From now on, the ecosystem itself, not the corporation *per se*, should serve as the point of departure for every business strategist seeking to understand the new economy—and for every manager, entrepreneur, and investor seeking to prosper in it.

Nor does the Internet tonic apply only to corporations. The web is dropping transaction costs everywhere—enabling networked approaches to almost every institution in society from government, media, science, and health care to our energy grid, transportation systems, and institutions for global problem solving.

Governments can change from being vertically integrated, industrial-age bureaucracies to become networks. By releasing their treasures of raw data, governments can now become platforms upon which companies, NGOs, academics, foundations, individuals, and other government agencies can collaborate to create public value.

If we listen to the theories of Mr. Coase from more than 60 years ago, we can understand how the digital revolution helps us find the uniquely qualified minds and talent to create wealth, to govern, and to educate ourselves for the future.

# TORONTO STAR

## First Nations need homegrown solution to poverty crisis

DON TAPSCOTT, TORONTO, ON, 4 NOVEMBER 2013: A.15

Despite the federal government pumping billions of dollars into housing, education, and health care on reserves throughout Canada, the standard of living of too many First Nations remains horrific, with rampant unemployment and substance abuse.

The Assembly of First Nations reports that a young person on a reserve is more likely to end up in jail than to graduate from high school. Suicide rates are five times higher than for young non-Aboriginal Canadians. The Aboriginal population is the fastest growing in Canada, with almost 40 per cent under the age of 20.

If you're like me, you're frustrated by the unrelenting challenges that seem to make it impossible for Aboriginal people to break the cycle of poverty, find decent jobs, and foster some sense of sustainable economic development. For my entire life, it has seemed like a never-ending problem with no way out. It doesn't make sense and it's impossible to believe it has to be that way.

So instead of doing more of the same, let's try making available to First Nations a Canadian resource that generates much of the prosperity that others enjoy. Let's try entrepreneurship.

Let's call on business owners and leaders across Canada to share their expertise with Aboriginal Canadians and provide them with the know-how to start and sustain their own businesses.

As we see in the rest of Canada, entrepreneurs are a source of innovation, growth, and prosperity. They bring fresh thinking to the marketplace and they fuel the creative destruction that makes market economies resilient.

Studies show that up to 80 per cent of new jobs come from companies that are five years old or less. Best of all, it's never been easier or cheaper to start a business than it is today, thanks to resources, knowledge, and networks available online.

But, as most entrepreneurs know, sage advice from a supportive mentor can make all the difference when navigating the stormy waters of a business's early years. Scores of organizations across the country, such as local chambers of commerce, make current or recently retired executives available to new business owners. These mentors provide invaluable moral support along with frank feedback and problem-solving advice.

Such support would be tremendously beneficial for Aboriginal entrepreneurs. I'm not suggesting that Toronto or Barrie business owners start flying into reserves in northwest Ontario. Thanks to the Internet, they don't have to leave their offices or living rooms. In 2013, you can coach an entrepreneur entirely online via email, social media, and Skype.

Building a national network of willing-and-able business mentors is what MentorNation—the brainchild of Toronto-based not-for-profit

Classroom Connections—is all about. It believes that experienced entrepreneurs, business people, and professionals would welcome the opportunity to do something practical about Aboriginal poverty.

MentorNation's role is to be the intermediary. It will create an online platform that matches business mentors with aspiring Aboriginal entrepreneurs. MentorNation hasn't built the online platform yet. That will happen next year. The first step is a pilot project to test the materials and processes to be used in the online platform. This includes training workshops to teach non-Aboriginal entrepreneurs how to work with their Aboriginal counterparts. Just as the organization is using the Internet to provide the mentoring, it is also using online tools to raise its operational funding. It wants to raise $200,000 in the next 33 days from ordinary Canadians. To do this, MentorNation is trying to gather the funds from the startup platform Giveffect.org. This is a new organization in Canada that wants to use crowdfunding to help Canadian charities.

Crowdfunding is fast becoming one of the most fascinating and important tools of economic change today, helping business startups and social enterprises. An individual or organization announces a target amount of money and what it would do with that money, and the public is asked to contribute online.

Individuals and new companies have used crowdfunding to raise billions of dollars in debt and equity during the past five years. In 2012, crowdfunding raised almost $2.7 billion (US) around the world, an 80 per cent increase over the year before.

You may recall the crowdfunding site Indiegogo. It gained fame in Toronto when Gawker used the site to collect $200,000 to buy the cellphone video that allegedly shows Mayor Rob Ford smoking what appeared to be crack cocaine.

Instead of donating money to watch the mayor on drugs, you can now donate money to help Aboriginal Canadians stay off drugs.

What I love about crowdfunding is that it is so much more than it seems at first blush. To view it simply as tapping friends and strangers for money misses most of the point. Instead, true crowdfunding should be an opportunity—an invitation to allow someone to be part of an exciting journey to collectively achieve something radical, new, and different. Its astonishing power lies in its exhilarating promise of change; its ability to empower ordinary people to accomplish a shared mission. It's motivational, it's fresh—and, most importantly, it works!

So the MentorNation campaign is not about donating money to a problem. It's about creating opportunity among First Nations for a homegrown solution, empowering individuals, and unleashing energy and optimism in people who have been waiting a long time.

2014

# Harvard Business Review

## A Bretton Woods for the 21st century

Don Tapscott, March 2014, Vol. 92, Issue 3, p. 40

If you are the leader of a large organization (or only of yourself ) who cares about improving the world, here's a question you should consider: How will you participate in the global solution networks that are increasingly managing to address the world's problems?

A global solution network is a group of independent parties that have coalesced around a global problem or task they all perceive as important but that none can handle on its own. They become a network when they begin communicating about and coordinating their activities to make progress, rather than working unilaterally and competitively (as, for example, an industry does in a market economy).

Cooperative efforts to solve shared problems have of course arisen in the past. In business the great examples have been standards networks. But the world's biggest social and economic ills have been addressed by gatherings of nation-states. The model for global cooperation was forged after World War II, when representatives of 44 countries met at Bretton Woods, New Hampshire; the work they did there led to the International Monetary Fund, the World Bank, the United Nations, the G8, the World Trade Organization, and more.

Once state-based institutions like these had taken hold, it became hard to imagine other ways to address territory-spanning social challenges—the human problems that, in the words of Kofi Annan, the former UN secretary-general, "do not come permanently attached to national passports." But over time it has also become clear that these institutions aren't equal to the task. Progress on many fronts is stalled.

Two major developments in recent decades have provided the basis for a new model. First, the Internet has created the means for participants of all sizes, down to individuals, to communicate, contribute resources, and coordinate action. We no longer need government officials to convene for the rest of us to align our goals and efforts. Second, businesses have gained the ability, by virtue of their international scale and their growing eagerness to be forces for good, to play an important role in global cooperative efforts. No businesses were at the table at Bretton Woods, but today corporations routinely engage with other sectors to address issues of sustainability, social justice, and public well-being.

Global solution networks lead to cooperation, governance, and problem solving—and make faster, stronger progress than state-based institutions ever could. If you doubt it, look at how the two models are dealing with climate change. State-based institutions have mobilized by meeting in Cancun, in Copenhagen, in Rio and have so far failed to align on a plan for even a 6 per cent reduction in carbon emissions. Meanwhile, some 20 million people have joined the Climate Reality Project and other self-organizing networks and are already taking action. Which is providing better leadership to save the planet?

As global solution networks proliferate (research at Rotman has already identified 10 types), business is ideally positioned to play an integral role. The challenge is clear: you now need to think strategically about which you will participate in and how. Will your organization act in isolation, talking on only problems that it can single-handedly solve? Or will you join the good fights taking place on a global scale, and leave the world meaningfully better?

# THE GLOBE AND MAIL

## Economic crisis continues for unemployed youth

DON TAPSCOTT, TORONTO, ON, 3 FEBRUARY 2014

## Opinion

In last week's State of the Union address, US president Barack Obama was quick to catalogue his economic successes.

But America's young are strikingly absent from the celebrations. They were the biggest factor in Mr. Obama winning the presidency. Today many feel betrayed, with youth unemployment more than double that of the general population.

This is a key reason the gap between the rich and the poor in the modern economy of the United States has never been greater. The president acknowledged such, saying, "The cold, hard fact is that even in the midst of recovery, too many Americans are working more than ever just to get by, let alone get ahead. And too many still aren't working at all."

This growing rich-poor disconnect was a major theme at the World Economic Forum meeting in Davos, which took place the week prior to Mr. Obama's speech. American chief executive officers attending Davos were ebullient about the economy, with Salesforce.com CEO Marc Benioff saying, "The economic crisis is over!" But in the next breath, Mr. Benioff pointed out there are looming concerns that could be devastating for business and humanity. The most important: "Automation is sucking jobs out of the economy."

In Davos, there was consensus that a new technology revolution is bringing some tectonic changes. We will go from two billion to six billion Internet users over the next decade, but that's just the beginning. Cisco Systems Inc.'s former chief executive John Chambers describes the next wave as "the Internet of Everything." Soon there will be trillions of objects online as the physical world around us becomes smart and networked.

The downside is that we may be entering an era of permanent structural unemployment in which, for the first time, economic growth does not generate jobs.

Former Google CEO Eric Schmidt said that we're into two or three decades in which jobs will be the dominant issue. Decades ago, a wave of computer-generated automation wiped out blue-collar jobs. This was followed by a wave of outsourcing that affected some white-collar workers. Now a new wave of robotics, networked-inspired automation, and new business models are targeted at knowledge work.

Technology is convulsing entire industries and wiping out professional and management jobs along with less-skilled ones.

Amazon.com Inc. turned book retailing on its head and is now transforming retailing itself, devastating big box stores like Best Buy (which recently laid off hundreds of Canadian employees). Parts of the magazine industry have been wiped out and newspapers are suffering. Bill Gates reported that he's working on robots that can pick crops better than humans can.

"This is a new phenomenon that is coming on very fast," Mr. Benioff said. Noting the epidemic of youth unemployment around the world, Cisco's former CEO Mr. Chambers said, "We're close to losing a generation of young people."

One essential ingredient to help grapple with these new problems is education. During the Industrial Revolution, people left the farms and the leaders of society understood that we needed public education. Today, there needs to be a similar revolution in education as we transition to the digital economy. For starters, when most workers are knowledge workers, most people will need postsecondary education. We also need to realign the capabilities of youth with the needs of labour markets. The biggest demand is for graduates in the so-called STEM: science, technology, engineering, and mathematics. Others argued that a key to overcoming the problem is entrepreneurship. Studies show that 80 per cent of new jobs come from companies five years old or less. Given the right conditions to take root and flourish, "gazelles," as Mr. Schmidt calls them, are the foundation of innovation, growth, and prosperity.

For many young people, being entrepreneurial and creating their own job will be the surest path to employment. If they've learned anything from the past six years, it's that they shouldn't rely on their elders.

# Toronto Star

## Firms must invest in job creation

Toronto, ON, 20 May 2014: A.14

**The misguided attack on arts and science degrees, Opinion, May 15**

Kudos to Don Tapscott for reminding us that "the purpose of education is not only to train workers," for if it were, education would be redundant. Still, as articulate and compelling as Tapscott's opinion piece may be, it makes a serious omission. Blaming arts and science colleges for failing to do what they are not primarily meant to do simply lets the real culprits off the hook. Employers are not just hoarding profits while failing to create jobs for graduates, deplorable in itself, but they are also failing to train their own employees. Even well-trained graduates need to be initiated to workplaces, something only employers themselves can do.

Rather than expecting Canadian universities to train students, we should be demanding that employers invest in job creation, and that they assume (rather than abdicate) the responsibility for training their own workers.

—Salvatore (Sal) Amenta, Stouffville

**There is no doubt the new economy is demanding a more highly skilled employee in almost every sector in the country.**

I'm not sure what Don Tapscott means by technical colleges, but Ontario's 24 public colleges offer a wide range of career-focused learning that earns students degrees, advanced diplomas, and diplomas.

To imply universities are the only place Canadians have access to critical thinking is a narrow view. There is a massive need for graduates who have a combination of soft skills such as problem solving and career-specific skills and qualifications to help them make an immediate contribution to the workplace. Colleges provide both.

I agree more resources should be allocated for postsecondary education but not just universities. As Canada moves toward a more highly skilled workforce, political leaders must place a greater emphasis on college education as part of a comprehensive strategy to produce a stronger workforce.

—LINDA FRANKLIN, PRESIDENT AND CEO OF COLLEGES
ONTARIO, TORONTO

# Toronto Star

## The solution revolution

Don Tapscott, Toronto, ON, 29 January 2014: A.17

If we reduce carbon emissions by a whopping 80 per cent by the year 2050, it will take a century for planet Earth to cool down. Despite our concerted efforts, this is the bleak point we've arrived at. It is estimated that within the next couple of decades two billion people will lose much of their water supply.

Climate change is one of dozens of pressing global problems nation-states have struggled to solve by working together through global institutions. Many of these organizations were created in the aftermath of the Second World War—beginning with a meeting of 42 countries in Bretton Woods, N.H. They include the International Monetary Fund, the World Bank, the United Nations, the G8 (Group of Eight), the World Trade Organization, and numerous other groups. For decades these institutions have wrestled with some of the world's most intractable problems—the kind of problems that don't fit neatly into departmental pigeonholes.

But progress has been slow or non-existent. Take climate change.

Today we are seeing the emergence of a new and fundamentally different way of tackling global problems. New non-state networks of private sector, civil society, government, and individual stake-holders are achieving new forms of cooperation and social change. They address every conceivable issue facing humanity, from poverty, human rights, health, and the environment, to economic policy, war, and even Internet governance.

Enabled by the digital revolution, these networks are now prolif-erating across the planet and are increasingly having an important impact. Call them global solution networks (GSNs).

GSNs depend on the cooperation of once-discrete sectors. There were no businesses at the table at Bretton Woods in 1944. But now business is being forced to become one of the "pillars of society."

Individual businesses are more aware than ever of the benefits of social responsibility. In the past, Corporate Social Responsibility advocates argued that companies "do well by doing good." But this wasn't always true. Many companies did well by doing bad—by having bad labour practices in the developing world, by externalizing their costs onto society by, for instance, polluting the environment. But in an increasingly transparent world, the adage about doing good is truer than ever. If it wasn't so before 2008, it certainly is now: companies "do badly by being bad."

There were only a few dozen NGOs at the time of Bretton Woods, and while some were in the room, they had no say.

Today the civil society is a major force, representing up to 15 per cent of the economy of some countries. And, increasingly, young people seek to do good in the workforce by becoming social entrepreneurs, creating new businesses that have a societal purpose on a mass scale.

In an age where everything and everyone is linked through networks of glass and air, no one—no business, organization, govern-ment agency, country—is an island. And no organization can succeed in a world that is failing.

GSNs, which have arisen from this world and are designed to respond to its problems, have four characteristics.

They involve civil society, business, and government; they attack a global problem; they make the most of the Internet and digital tools; and they are not controlled by states or corporations. These networks engage tens of thousands of organizations and tens of millions of people on a daily basis.

And we are already seeing the influence of GSNs on international policy. For instance, for the first time, thousands of businesses were invited to participate in the Climate Change Summit in Warsaw in 2013. Meanwhile, hundreds of advocacy networks such as the Alliance for Climate Change are working to educate, mobilize, and change government policies.

GSNs take many forms and serve many functions. Some, like Ushahidi, are platforms for those who seek change—websites that allow people to share information and organize around a cause. Some, like the International Competition Network, create policies for companies and governments. Some, like Human Rights Watch, are funded by corporations and philanthropists and scrutinize the behaviour of governments everywhere. Some, like TED, create unprecedented access to global information and ideas. Some, such as the World Economic Forum or the Clinton Global Network, resemble more traditional state-based institutions in the scope of their mandate, but unlike those institutions are self-organizing, not controlled by governments.

Incredibly, GSNs can manage resources, too. It is a diffuse GSN, more than any collection of states, that governs the Internet. This year's September conference on climate change will be a true multi-stakeholder network comprising business and civil society, which may eventually yield a GSN to govern carbon emissions.

As we go forward, global problem solving and governance will be co-owned by a variety of stakeholders, including corporations. Global governance is not owned by any one governing body. It is becoming a challenge owned by all of us.

# LinkedIn

## (Almost) everything we think about managing millennials is wrong. Here's why.

### Don Tapscott, 28 October 2014

Today's workplace should look more like a jazz band (yes, that's a pic of me) rather than a Dilbert-style bureaucracy that looks more like a dysfunctional marching band. As Dilbert pointed out (in the best-selling management book of all time) our approach to talent management is deeply flawed.

But meaningful change is beginning to happen. The digital revolution is enabling new models of collaboration that lead to better innovation and higher performance. A new generation of young workers (the Millennials or the Net Generation as I've called them) is entering the workforce and bringing a new culture. And the new business environment demands something better. This requires a rethinking of talent management.

The current model of talent management is recruit, train, manage, retain, and evaluate the performance of employees. In the future smart companies won't do any of this. Work will look more like a jazz ensemble where hierarchy is replaced by creativity, sense-and-respond, peer-to-peer, collaboration, empowerment, and improvisation.

## 1. Don't recruit: Initiate relationships and engage the best talent.

In the old model of human resources, potential new hires were solicited using one-way broadcast advertising methods, such as newspaper classified ads. Today, advertising to attract young people is a waste of time and money. Companies can use social media to influence this generation about their company and get to know them.

Old-style job interviews were much like interrogations in which potential employees were grilled on their strengths and weaknesses, knowledge and skills, sometimes being asked to perform tests that are terrible predictors of effectiveness. This approach should be completely revised. Employers who seek to identify, attract, and hire the best talent should see the process as a dialogue.

And starting early, even in high school, companies can use challenges, projects, part-time jobs, internships, summer employment, and the like to get to know the best and brightest. When it's time to hire them, there is no "recruiting" to be done, as you have already engaged the people you want. It's simply a boundary change, where you bring your collaborator inside the boundaries of your firm.

## 2. Don't train: Create work-learning environments.

Working and learning in the knowledge economy are basically the same thing. What are you doing right now reading this book? Working or learning? So rather than sending off employees to separate training and educational activities, why not use the new media to increase the learning component of their work? Rather than training them, engage them in rich working-learning environments for lifelong learning.

At my company, our "training" strategy is three words: "Everyone must blog." In doing so, everyone learns how to research, write well, defend his or her ideas, and collaborate and engage with the world.

The Net Generation in particular will respond well if mentored and coached to contribute to corporate policies, strategy, and business performance. Thus, employers must use creativity and flexibility when organizing the first few months of work to expose the new employees to various leaders, work situations, and work content. Greater transparency of, exposure to, and interactivity with the broader organization during this initiation phase will lead to a win-win outcome. Companies that make the effort will benefit from less turnover, shorter ramp-up speeds, higher levels of engagement, and earlier and greater returns on their investments in employees.

How could your company increase the learning component of work?

## 3. Don't manage: Collaborate.

The Dilbertian enterprise is divided into the governors and the governed. At the top is the supreme governor and at the bottom the permanently governed. In between are those that alternate. These bureaucracies are slow. Employees are supervised and isolated in silos where knowledge is not shared.

Increasingly, traditional approaches to supervision and management are not effective. Good managers build teams and engage employees through distributing authority, power, and accountability. A growing number of firms are decentralizing their decision-making function, communicating in a peer-to-peer fashion, and embracing new technologies that empower employees to communicate easily and openly with people inside and outside the firm. In doing so, they are creating a new corporate meritocracy that is sweeping away the hierarchical silos in its path and connecting internal teams to a wealth of external networks.

Collaboration is a two-way street. Work styles, workflow models, workday and workplace parameters, career paths, and professional development offerings should be examined and potentially retooled by organizations to maximize fit with the generational mix of employees.

How could your company move from a supervision model to one of true collaboration?

## 4. Don't retain: Evolve lasting relationships.

In today's volatile work environment, you can't retain talent like you retain fluids.

Talent doesn't need to be inside the boundaries of your enterprise. The Internet drops transaction and collaboration costs and companies can find uniquely qualified minds to create value anywhere. This opens a new world of relationships between talent and firms. Using the analogy of the university's alumni network, companies should think of employees as a web of contacts. They should be perceived as networks, with a wealth of knowledge about the company's inner workings, which possess the opportunity to add great value, even after leaving the company. Social networking, communities of practice, and other web platforms allow employees and ex-employees alike to exchange resources and disseminate information. Net Generation employees will embrace this kind of thinking as it comes naturally to them, having grown up on online communities such as Facebook.

Some of my best talent is not inside the boundaries of my company. How could your company become a network rather than a fortress for talent?

## 5. Don't do annual reviews: Improve performance real time.

If you're a manager, you may have noticed that your 20-something employees need plenty of feedback. It's part of their mind-set and is honed by a lifetime of immersion in interactive digital technologies. This has had a profound effect on the Net Generation's mental habits and their way of doing things. They've grown up to expect two-way conversation, not lectures from a parent, teacher, or employer. They're used to constant and quick feedback from friends about everything—their homework, a new gadget, and now their job.

The annual performance appraisal, in which the boss tells the underling how he or she rates against corporate objectives, makes little sense for young employees. It's often a one-way "appraisal"— boss to employee—that usually downplays the employee's wishes and desires. It happens once a year—long after the performance took place. It rewards or punishes individual performance—not the collaboration that the new workforce treasures. It's more about compensation and promotions than about improving performance.

So how do you give feedback to a generation that has an insatiable desire for it? How do you do it in a way that makes sense to people under 30?

There are new software packages, such as Work.com, that offer tools to enable real-time feedback. Instead of waiting an entire year to find out what managers think of them, employees can send out a quick (50 words or fewer) question to people they trust—a manager, a co-worker sitting in the meeting, even a client, or a supplier. Baby boomers like me still wonder whether software like this will make our email inboxes overflow with requests for "advice." But I think managers will stop complaining once they see that employees are using this information to quickly improve their performance.

# HARVARD BUSINESS REVIEW

## After 20 years, it's harder to ignore the digital economy's dark side

DON TAPSCOTT, 11 MARCH 2016

In 1995, I published *The Digital Economy*, a book that became one of the first bestsellers about the Internet in business. To mark its 20th anniversary, my publisher asked me to write a dozen minichapters for a new edition. As I revisited it, I was struck by how far we've come since 1995 and by how many concepts in the book have withstood the test of time. "The digital economy" term itself has become part of the vernacular.

The book was pretty breathless about the opportunities of the digital revolution, but it equally warned of some huge dangers ahead—and this dark side has indeed emerged over the last two decades. Back then, I wrote:

> The Age of Networked Intelligence is also an age of peril. For individuals, organizations, and societies that fall behind, punishment is swift. It is not just old business rules but

also governments, social institutions, and relationships among people that are being transformed. The new media is changing the ways we do business, work, learn, play, and even think. Far more than the old western frontier, the digital frontier is a place of recklessness, confusion, uncertainty, calamity, and danger.

Some signs point to a new economy in which wealth is even further concentrated, basic rights like privacy are vanishing, and a spiral of violence and repression undermine basic security and freedoms. Pervasive evidence exists that indicates the basic social fabric is beginning to disintegrate. Old laws, structures, norms, and approaches are proving to be completely inadequate for life in the new economy. While they are crumbling or being smashed, it is not completely clear what should replace them. Everywhere people are beginning to ask, "Will this smaller world our children inherit be a better one?"

While the digital revolution has brought us many wonders, in hindsight my somewhat discouraging conclusion is that the "promise" of a more fair, equal, just, and sustainable world has been unfulfilled. It has become clear that the original democratic architecture of the Internet has been bent to the will of economies and societies in which power is anything but distributed. If anything, the power has become more concentrated, and the main benefits of the digital economy have been skewed.

Let's look at a few concerns I raised in 1995 and assess what has actually happened in the years since.

## "Dislocations in labour markets, with old industries and jobs disappearing."

In the book, I warned that technology might actually destroy more jobs than it was creating. I asked, "How will we manage the transition to new types of work and a new knowledge base for the economy?"

Now, for the first time in modern history, economic growth in OECD countries is not generating a commensurate number of new jobs. Young workers are taking the biggest hit. Arguably, structural unemployment will be the biggest public policy issue for decades.

It appears that the biggest culprit is digital technologies themselves. We've already seen knowledge work such as accounting and legal services being shipped offshore to cheaper employees. Soon the work will stay here but be done by computers. For example, IBM's Watson computer diagnoses cancers with much higher levels of speed and accuracy than skilled physicians do. The same software combined with robotics, 3D printing, and myriad other innovations will continue to eliminate jobs throughout the workforce. Technology is also the foundation of new species of businesses that are capable of wiping out entire industries. Spectacular digital conglomerates such as Apple, Google, Amazon, and others are taking over a dozen industries, partly because they do a better job with a fraction of the employees. Service aggregators such as Uber, Lyft, and Airbnb hold the power to wipe out jobs in transportation and hospitality industries. Data frackers such as Facebook are acquiring vast troves of data that position them to dominate multiple industries.

Factoring in the hangover from the financial collapse of 2008, we're witnessing youth unemployment levels across the Western world from 15 to 50 per cent. This situation is not only immoral; it is creating a massive powder keg. Rather than a Schumpeterian "creative destruction," we're seeing structural elimination of entire labour markets.

## "The destruction of privacy in an unprecedented and irrevocable manner."

I believed this topic to be so important that I devoted an entire chapter to it. I wrote: "Most of us believe we have the right to decide what personal information we divulge, to whom, and for what purpose. Left unchecked, the Internet could render such thinking irrelevant."

Safeguarding privacy is now a major concern on people's minds. So-called data minimization, or limiting what information we give away, is no longer feasible. Everywhere we go and in everything we do, we leave a trail of digital crumbs. Today, what happens in Vegas, stays...on YouTube.

Rather than restricting what we input, every country needs better norms and laws protecting our privacy. For example, we should own the data we create. And if we give it to social media companies, it should only be used for the purpose for which it was collected—not sold to others without our permission.

## "The danger of growing social inequality."

Two decades ago, the book warned of a "severe bipolarization of wealth" that could foster a two-tiered society where the benefits of the digital age are asymmetrical and where wealth creation does not lead to prosperity for all.

Today, income inequality is one of the hottest topics on the planet. It was listed as the number-one global risk by the World Economic Forum's 2014 meeting in Davos, Switzerland. It is the subject of *Capital in the Twenty-First Century*, the *New York Times* bestseller by French economist Thomas Piketty. While many people disagree with his socialist conclusions, Piketty's scholarship has been pretty much unassailable, showing that growing social inequality is endemic to capitalism, even in the digital age. More people today are questioning whether the digital revolution might actually accelerate inequality.

## "Many governments seem slow to comprehend the shift."

In 1995, I wrote, "Bureaucracies by definition resist change, thinking that heads-down is the route to survival. Can government become electronic, transforming the way government services are delivered?"

Have the operations of governments changed fundamentally in the past two decades? Sure, there are improvements, but most governments have spent time making existing models of government digital—paving the cow path—instead of rethinking the system in a digital age. (The same applies to many legacy businesses that are struggling with their digital transformations but lack market forces to compel change.) The economic crisis of 2008 has made it more urgent for governments to think seriously about both how they can use open data and social media to alter the deep structures of government and how we orchestrate capability to create public value.

## "What will happen to democracy?"

These questions are still relevant today: "Will the electronic town hall become an electronic mob? Will cyberdemocracy become hyperdemocracy? Or can we craft a new age in which networked intelligence can be applied for the good of the people?"

The problem is hardly too much citizen engagement through digital media, as I worried; the opposite is occurring. Industrial-age governments have clung to the "you vote, I rule" model, where politicians broadcast their views to passive citizens. This is leading to a crisis of legitimacy among democratic institutions (of which the US Congress is Exhibit A). This matters. Seymour Martin Lipset, the American political sociologist, wrote that legitimacy is "the capacity of a political system to engender and maintain the belief that existing political institutions are the most appropriate and proper ones for the society."

The ongoing abuse of trust by office holders is not simply a series of isolated incidents; it is the manifestation of a deep and widespread rot. And people have had it. During the past 20 years, voter turnout has dropped in most Western democracies, particularly among young people, who are looking for alternative ways to bring about social change.

To restore legitimacy and trust, we need to do what *The Digital Economy* advised two decades ago: build a second era of democracy based on integrity and accountability, with stronger, more open institutions, active citizenship, and a culture of public discourse and participation.

## Going forward

Technological utopians are being proven wrong by the facts: technology does not create prosperity, good democracy, and justice—humans do. To ensure that the digital economy fulfills its promise, we'll need a new social contract that guarantees opportunities for full employment, protects our privacy, and enables prosperity not just for the few but for everyone.

# ROTMAN MAGAZINE

## Thought leader interview: Don Tapscott

KAREN CHRISTENSEN, SPRING 2016

**You have said that the modern corporation is in the midst of a "perfect storm." Please explain.**

Four drivers are transforming the modern enterprise as we know it. The first is a new paradigm in technology that includes the social web, Big Data, the Internet of Things, cloud computing, robotics, machine learning, and mobility. And there is much more to come. The next stage of the Internet will be based on the underlying technology of Bitcoin: the blockchain is a globally distributed database of potentially *all* structured information, and it holds profound implications for the architecture of the corporation and how we create goods and services.

The second change is demographic—but it's not about the aging population, as most people think. Rather, it's about the young generation of digital natives that has now entered the workforce—bringing with them the desire for a culture of innovation, speed, customization, freedom, integrity, and collaboration. There is no

---

more powerful force out there to change most of what we know about talent management.

The third driver is economic, and it has to do with the continuing struggles of the global economy as the industrial age comes to an end, and new requirements emerge for competiveness and prosperity. For the first time in modern history, the 51st percentile of individuals and families is not getting ahead. Throughout decades of economic change, wars—even depressions—this group has always managed to progress, but that is not happening today. There are big issues on the table about how to compete through innovation and create prosperity for not just a few—but for everyone.

The fourth driver is the arrival of new business models that are unlike anything we've seen before. Digital conglomerates like Alphabet, Amazon, and Apple are rapidly evolving into adjacent and not-so-adjacent industries; then there are "data frackers" like Facebook and Dataminr that do "horizontal mining" for data. At the same time, we're seeing the wave of service aggregators like Uber and Airbnb. These are just a few examples of new models that are shaking the windows and rattling the doors of traditional business structures; through blockchain technology, they are about to be disrupted, as well.

When you put all of this together, "perfect storm" is probably an understatement for what businesses are facing.

## What skills are required to lead in this environment?

The concept of leadership is changing. Peter Senge was right when he argued, 25 years ago, that the person at the top cannot be expected to learn for the organization as a whole anymore. Things have become too complicated, and leaders must proactively create a "learning organization." It is now possible—and important—for people throughout an organization to behave as leaders, and the new collaborative systems that are being designed actually call for this. Talent and leadership from throughout your organization—and even from outside of it—must be harnessed.

The old-fashioned, Lee Iacocca model of the leader as a visionary who sells his vision down through an organization is being replaced by a much more collaborative and trustworthy model. This doesn't mean that there isn't a role for vision, but today, the best visions are collectively created.

**You believe that the wicked problems the world faces can be addressed—but that progress has stalled, because we are using the wrong model. Please explain.**

There is no doubt that the world is a very troubled place: it is unsustainable, unequal, conflicted, and unjust. If you look at the top 20 problems facing humanity, some of them are getting better. For instance, poverty in the developed world has gone from one dollar a day to two dollars a day. Yet half of the world's population is still living on under ten dollars a day—so how excited can we get about that? With problems like conflict, it's hard to say whether it's getting better or not, and some problems are definitely getting worse. Climate change, for instance, has begun to take some significant tolls. For the last few decades, the way we have approached these problems is through nation-states, working together in global institutions. This approach began seriously at Bretton Woods in 1944, after the Second World War, when we created the World Bank and the International Monetary Fund. A year later, a broader group created the United Nations and then

UNESCO, the GATT, the World Trade Organization, the G20 and the G8.

The trouble is, collaboration among nation-states—while still necessary—is now insufficient. Since Bretton Woods, there have been some profound changes to the economic environment: the rise of the corporation as a pillar of society; the emergence of a civil society (which didn't really exist in 1944); and the Internet, which dramatically drops transaction and collaboration costs on a global basis. These changes have enabled a new model to emerge: multi-stakeholder networks—or, as my colleagues and I call them, global solution networks (GSNs).

In some cases, GSNs can govern resources on behalf of the planet. The Internet, for example, is governed by a rag-tag ecosystem of global solution networks rather than by nation-states. If we can govern the Internet in this way, what else could we govern? The climate? Perhaps.

## You have identified 10 types of global solution networks. Which has the greatest potential?

The most interesting one to me is the governance network, whereby companies, governments at all levels, civil society organizations, NGOs, foundations, academics, and other individuals cooperate together to solve a global problem. Governance networks combine a series of other GSNs like knowledge networks, advocacy networks, platforms, policy networks, diasporas, watchdog networks, networked institutions, and standards networks.

Old-growth forests are now being governed through such a network, as is the issue of conflict diamonds. These networks are also attacking problems like child pornography and child predators on the Internet—issues that cannot be addressed within the context of a nation-state, because they are *global* in nature. By far, the most exciting thing to me is that we are seeing the emergence of a governance network that could actually oversee the world's climate. We are in the early days of a mobilization of the entire planet Earth that is very different from the last two such mobilizations—which were world wars. With this mobilization, all of the world would potentially be on the same side. It turns out that the "killer app" for global solution networks may be saving the planet—literally.

## 10 Types of Global Solution Networks:

Knowledge Networks | Policy Networks | Networked Institutions Governance Networks | Global Standards Networks | Advocacy Networks Operational & Delivery Networks | Platforms | Diasporas | Watchdog Networks

### Introducing: The Blockchain

The Internet, as it is currently designed, is not all that good for doing business, let alone the peer-to-peer business that can democratize prosperity and engage the world's population more directly in the global economy.

Overall, it has enabled many positive changes—for those with access to it. But without an economic layer to the Net, we can't establish each other's identity or trust each other to make transactions without validation from a third party like a bank or a government. Quite the opposite: the Internet allows people to commit fraud, collect our data, and invade our privacy; it excludes 2.5 billion people from the global financial system; and it channels power and prosperity to those who already have it, even if they are no longer earning it.

The next generation of the Internet can be the key to solving these problems. The digital revolution is bringing a new and radically different platform for business and other institutions that can take us through the next quarter-century of human progress. At the core of this is a piece of software ingenuity that may surprise you. It is the technology underlying the digital currency Bitcoin, known simply as the blockchain. This technology platform is open and programmable and therefore holds the potential to unleash countless new applications—of which Bitcoin is one—and as-yet-unrealized capabilities that have the potential to transform everything in the next 25 years.

At its most basic, the blockchain is a global spreadsheet—an incorruptible digital ledger of economic transactions that can be programmed to record not just financial transactions, but virtually everything of value and importance to humankind: birth and death certificates, marriage licences, deeds and titles of ownership, educational degrees, financial accounts, medical procedures, insurance claims, votes, transactions between "smart" objects, and anything else that can be expressed in code. This ledger represents the truth because mass collaboration constantly reconciles it. We will not need to trust each other in the traditional sense, because this new platform ensures integrity.

**Don Tapscott** and **Alex Tapscott**
EXCERPTED FROM THEIR *HUFFINGTON POST* BLOG, MARCH 2015

**Earlier, you touched on the focus of your latest work: blockchain technology. Please describe some of the changes it will bring.**

Basically, the Internet is entering a second era, providing us with another kick at the can to achieve a prosperous future. The blockchain is a truly open, distributed, global "ledger of the truth" that will fundamentally change what we can achieve online, how we do it, and who can participate.

When you think about the impact of the first few decades of the Internet, lots of good things have happened, but there have also been negative effects: social inequality has increased; we are losing our basic right to privacy; and we are facing a period of structural unemployment—largely caused by technology.

In the old technology paradigm—broadcasting and print—there was centralized control by powerful sources, and the recipients were passive. The new paradigm was supposed to be controlled by everyone, and to empower active participants. However, the Internet was dropped into an economy with concentrated power structures with an asymmetrical ability to shape it for their own purposes. As a result, wealth, prosperity, and freedom have arrived—but only for a few.

What if there were a next generation of the Internet, where we could conduct peer-to-peer transactions—not just to exchange information, but to exchange value and money? We can't do that today without a powerful intermediary—like a credit card company or PayPal. If we could create commerce without powerful intermediaries, there would be unlimited potential for creating a more prosperous and just world.

Today, 70 per cent of the world's people who own a small piece of land have tenuous rights to that land because powerful forces can declare that they don't own it. Over time, all land registry could be placed on the blockchain—this distributed database of all structured information that is incorruptible and unhackable. That way, no dictator could say, "You don't own this land; my friend does."

What if half a trillion dollars in remittance from the world's diasporas—people who have left their ancestral lands to work and send money home to their relatives—didn't go into transaction fees but was actually sent to the people who needed the money? What if we could create companies with tens of millions of shareholders by holding Kickstarter-like campaigns on the blockchain? What if musicians, rather than receiving crumbs at the end of the food chain for the value they create, got fed first by posting their music with associated rights and contracts on the blockchain? Those are just a few of dozens of examples of how this technology could be transformative.

## Given all of the above, are you optimistic about the future?

I am mainly because of the coming blockchain revolution. As indicated, the first era of the digital age has not fully delivered on its promise. We will soon have another opportunity to rewrite the economic order of things and dramatically improve the state of the world.

# TORONTO STAR

## Innovation

DON TAPSCOTT, TORONTO, ON, 7 MAY 2016: A.1

Canada is at a turning point. Plummeting oil prices, lacklustre economic performance, a petrodollar, pernicious climate change, and structural youth unemployment illustrate the need for a shift from a resource economy appropriate for the industrial age to an innovation economy appropriate for the digital age.

Toronto, specifically, can lead the way and become a global centre for innovation, entrepreneurship, breakthrough science, rich culture, open government, and prosperity as a whole.

In this special innovation edition of the *Star*, I've helped curate stories outlining mind-boggling developments, and even written a few, in the hope that you will become motivated to join in, if you haven't already.

The Canadian economy has been based on resources and traditional industrial-age manufacturing and approaches. It's time to move forward. This is not to say we should abandon our resource industries or manufacturing. They are also changing through innovation. If we do this right, they can become cleaner, safer, and better for everyone.

In the industrial age, powerful institutions produced standard-ized goods and services that were sent to passive participants. They pumped out consumer goods, TV shows, advertisements, govern-ment services, movies, cars, and even solutions to global problems. Teachers pushed out lectures. Clinicians delivered health care. Police officers delivered public safety to people who gratefully received it.

Now, thanks to the digital revolution, we can all become engaged and co-create our economy, communities, and city. Collaboration changes everything.

We can no longer count on big resource companies, manufactur-ers, or banks to create jobs. Entrepreneurship creates jobs and we need to foster that. Toronto has the talent to be the most vibrant hub of invention, creation, and innovation in the world. We need collaboration applied to areas such as innovative models of industry, education, health care, government, and democracy.

Canada has healthy, powerful, and well-run banks. However, their executives will tell you that new financial technologies, so-called fintech, are beginning to revolutionize financial services and they're gearing up for big changes.

You will read about the most important technology bringing change in banking and many other parts of the city and country—the blockchain revolution. Blockchain is enabling the Internet to enter a second era where we can establish trust to do transactions and conduct business and human affairs without powerful interme-diaries like banks, governments, or technology companies, but rather through mass collaboration and clever code. We need to think differ-ently about transportation. Within a decade, self-driving cars will be everywhere and if we plan today, we can have a virtual mass transit system for a tiny fraction of the cost of industrial-age approaches.

Perhaps it's even time for regional models of governance embracing exciting new green mini-cities like the proposed East Harbour, a 60-acre commercial development project planned for Toronto and expected to create 50,000 new jobs.

We need stronger communities where public safety is delivered not just by police but by all of us collaborating through networks and where big data is the criminal's worst nightmare.

Imagine a city where, in 2025, technology eliminates most of the challenges for people with disabilities. Let's embrace artificial intelligence for medicine, build bionic bones, create an Internet of DNA, and shift scientific research to a collaborative model rather than what exists today. Let's use DNA testing to ensure food safety and 3D-print missing body parts.

Culture is changing, too, as exemplified by the Toronto International Film Festival, which has undertaken bold efforts to transform itself for the networked age, leveraging digital technologies such as an online screening platform and awarding change makers in the industry.

Imagine open government—not just transparency but governments that share their data with citizens and engage us through exciting new techniques like challenges, digital brainstorms, and policy wikis. Let's move to a new era in democracy with active citizenship and a culture of public deliberation and elected representatives that act with integrity.

This is not a time for tinkering with old approaches. It's a time of transformation. Toronto and Canada both need an innovation strategy and it is my hope that this issue of the *Star* will act as a catalyst.

The strategy shouldn't be created just by government, but also by the private sector, NGOs, academia, cultural groups, and communities. It needs to be created by us all, and cultivated by you.

# Toronto Star

## Coming together to address global issues

Don Tapscott, Toronto, ON, 7 May 2016: B.4

Historically, societies have attempted to solve global problems through states working together through institutions like the UN.

Nongovernmental organizations (NGOs) also helped through advocating change, by mobilizing, or through volunteerism. Companies went about their business of winning customers and making money. Some companies contributed through philanthropy or through their corporate social responsibility (CSR) initiatives. But progress has been slow.

However, in assessing the world of global conflict, growing social inequality, climate change, economic malaise, and myriad other global problems, a growing number of corporate leaders understand that business can't succeed in a world that's failing.

The good news is that there is a powerful new way that business can now effectively contribute to a better world by creating and connecting multi-stakeholder networks. Together, companies, NGOs, governments, researchers, and other individuals are carving out a new and powerful way to affect global change.

Thanks to the Internet and some big changes in the global economy, everyone can leverage the effects of networks to create a dramatically bigger impact than previously thought possible, while at the same time advancing their commercial interests. This is not only good, it's necessary.

There is something new on the scene, and by the year 2025 this may in fact be the main way we seek to build a better world.

A global solution network is a group of independent parties that have been brought together by a world problem they all perceive to be important and that no single group has the ability to handle on its own. They become a network when they begin communicating about coordinating their activities to make progress, rather than working independently and competitively (as an "industry" in a market economy).

There are knowledge networks such as Wikipedia, Galaxy Zoo, and TED (for Technology, Entertainment, and Design) and advocacy networks such as Kony 2012, mobilizing tens of millions of people to change policy. Then we have policy networks such as the International Competition Network determining policy for global institutions and governments. Human Rights Watch and Transparency International are watchdog networks as they perform an oversight role, while networks that govern important resources—like the ecosystem that runs the Internet worldwide—are called governance networks. Large global institutions such as the World Economic Forum draw on vast networking capabilities from all 10 types.

Cooperative, multi-stakeholder efforts to solve shared problems have arisen in the past. In business, the most apparent examples have been "standards networks."

Yet historically, the world's biggest social and economic ills have been predominantly addressed by gatherings of countries. Remarkably, the model we still have and use for global political and economic cooperation was forged in the aftermath of the Second World War, when 42 countries convened at Bretton Woods, N.H., and created the United Nations, International Monetary Fund, World Bank, G8, World Trade Organization, and more.

Once state-based institutions like these took hold, it became hard to imagine that there could be other ways to address territory-spanning social challenges. These are the human problems that transcend borders. But over time, it has become clear that these institutions acting alone are unequal to the tasks we set them at Bretton Woods. Progress on many fronts has stalled.

Two major developments in recent decades have provided the basis for the new model.

First, the advent of the Internet has created the means for enterprises of all sizes down to the individual to communicate, contribute resources, and coordinate action. We no longer need government officials to convene in order for the rest of us to align our goals and efforts.

Second, businesses have gained the ability, perhaps by virtue of a newly international consumer base or a growing eagerness to be forces for good, to play an important role in global cooperative efforts. There were no businesses at the table at Bretton Woods. But today, corporations routinely engage with other sectors to address issues in sustainability, social justice, and public well-being.

Consider the process of addressing climate change by regulating greenhouse gas emissions. We're in the early days of a new approach that goes beyond national governments and engages all facets of society. At the annual UN Climate Change Conference that took place last fall in Paris (COP21), talks were aimed at a successor agreement to the now-expired Kyoto Protocol. The conference was particularly unique in that it convened more than 750 participants from across business, government, investors, NGOs, the UN, and civil society.

The Kyoto Protocol, on the other hand, extended the 1992 UN Framework Convention on Climate Change, committing parties to reduce greenhouse gas emissions and engaging only states in the process.

Countries remain essential. They're needed to write and enforce the domestic laws required to give an international agreement teeth. But the overall battle can only be won if businesses, local and regional governments, power providers, transportation systems, other institutions, and billions of citizens get involved.

We need to mobilize the resources of humanity on a scale not dissimilar to what we saw during the two world wars, but this time we will all be fighting together and for the same cause.

The combination of these developments yields a new model. Global solution networks, as opposed to state-based institutions acting in isolation, can achieve global cooperation, governance, and problem solving—and make it a faster, stronger progress than non-networked state-based institutions ever could.

The challenge is clear: you now need to think strategically about which you will participate in, and how.

Will your organization act in isolation, taking on only the size of problems it can single-handedly solve? Or will you join the good and many fights taking place on a global scale, and leave the world meaningfully better?

Chancellor Don Tapscott greets guests attending the Chancellor's dinner celebrating award winners during convocation. *Photo courtesy of Trent University.*

Don Tapscott speaking to guests attending the Toronto book launch of *Blockchain Revolution* at the Rotman School of Management, University of Toronto, in 2016. At the time Don was also an adjunct professor at the Rotman School of Management. *Photo courtesy of Don Tapscott.*

(L to R) Chancellor Don Tapscott and Trent University's Sarah Gallen at the Chancellor Lecture Series "Blockchain Revolution—How the Technology Behind Bitcoin Is Changing Money, Business, and the World" on November 22, 2016, at Trent University Durham in Oshawa, Ontario. During this lecture, Chancellor Don Tapscott discussed his book *Blockchain Revolution* and explained why blockchain technology will fundamentally transform the way we move, store, and manage value online. Following the lecture, he signed books for audience members. *Photo courtesy of Trent University.*

(L to R) Honorary Esquire Bedel Cpl Girard (of the Hastings and Prince Edward Regiment), President and Vice-Chancellor Leo Groarke, and Chancellor Don Tapscott in the procession of the Community Parade on October 18, 2014, in downtown Peterborough, Ontario. This parade during Trent University's 50th anniversary celebrated the contributions of the Peterborough community in the founding of Trent University. The parade reenacted the original processional parade from the opening ceremonies of Trent University in 1964. *Photo courtesy of Trent University.*

Event poster for the Chancellor Lecture Series: "Blockchain Revolution—How the Technology Behind Bitcoin Is Changing Money, Business, and the World" on November 22, 2016, at Trent University Durham in Oshawa, ON. During this lecture, Chancellor Don Tapscott discussed his new book *Blockchain Revolution* and explained why blockchain technology—an open, distributed, global platform—will fundamentally transform the way we move, store, and manage value online. *Poster courtesy of Trent University.*

Event poster for the Chancellor Lecture Series "Towards a New Social Contract for the Digital Age" on November 16, 2018, at Trent University in Peterborough, Ontario. Dr. Len Epp interviewed Chancellor Don Tapscott for a special episode of the Leanpub Frontmatter podcast. Topics discussed included the crisis of legitimacy of our democratic institutions and the generational divide along technological lines, among others. *Poster courtesy of Trent University.*

(L to R) The Honourable Elizabeth Dowdeswell, OC OOnt, Lieutenant Governor of Ontario, and Chancellor Don Tapscott, CM, at the Chancellor's Gala during Trent University's 50th anniversary on October 17, 2014. Attended by alumni, donors, community members, and dignitaries, the Chancellor's Gala celebrated 50 years of excellence at Trent University with a variety of speakers and performers. *Photo courtesy of Trent University.*

(L to R) Chancellor Don Tapscott and founding President of Trent University Professor Thomas H.B. Symons on June 8, 2018. Trent University graduates from the first two classes (1964 and 1965) were invited to join the ceremony to celebrate the 50th anniversary of the first convocation ceremony. *Photo courtesy of Trent University.*

(L to R) CTV National News anchor Lisa Laflamme interviewed Chancellor Emeritus Don Tapscott live at Trent University on September 13, 2019. At the start of the federal election campaign, Trent University took centre stage in a national CTV News broadcast, which also included interviews with students. *Photo courtesy of Trent University.*

Trent University convocation ceremonies are held outside in front of the Bata library, beside the Otonabee River in Peterborough, Ontario. *Photo courtesy of Trent University.*

(L to R) David Moore, Joan Moore, Curve Lake First Nation Elder Doug Williams, Chancellor Don Tapscott, and founding President of Trent University Professor Thomas H.B. Symons at the Bata Library transformation celebration on November 16, 2018, in Peterborough, Ontario. The multimillion dollar project was celebrated with Trent students, faculty, staff, alumni, donors, and community members. Chancellor Don Tapscott, other dignitaries, and special guests unveiled the new spaces and amenities. *Photo courtesy of Trent University.*

# TORONTO STAR

## TIFF's future starts with an app

TONY WONG, TORONTO, ON, 7 MAY 2016: E.5

Author and consultant Don Tapscott worked with the Toronto International Film Festival (TIFF) to determine how the organization could innovate.

But before the festival starts to build on its global presence, it still has to walk before it can fly, warns Tapscott.

That includes starting with the basics: building a better app that will allow truly seamless integration for festival goers.

"I have the same gripes that everyone does. The transactions are confusing. It's time-consuming and then there are lineups, when all you want to do is enjoy the film," says Tapscott.

Companies such as Starbucks, for example, have apps that allow customers to order a coffee and have it waiting when they get to the shop. Why can't TIFF be that easy?

"The app is your virtual co-pilot to TIFF," says Tapscott. "It should be like a combination of having a great executive assistant and Martin Scorsese in your pocket to guide you through the festival."

Here are some other suggestions taken from Tapscott's internal report in a collaboration that started in 2012 with the film festival.

# Partnering with online broadcasters

TIFF can expand its reach by partnering with companies such as Netflix, iTunes, and Amazon. TIFF's library of red-carpet moments, panels, and interviews can be used to supplement broadcast material such as the extras found on DVDs.

# Creating community

TIFF can engage communities of film lovers globally—integrating existing online and face-to-face groups into the TIFF community that already exist through Meetup.com, Facebook, and others. TIFF should be able to increase its public profile, attract fans, and be community friendly.

# Crowdsourcing film series

What kind of series would you like to see at TIFF? The organization could ask fans to rate their favourite films and stars, then build a series theme around that. Crowdsourcing merchandise and design is another option, with TIFF partnering with design schools, which will help raise public awareness and link with other artistic partners.

# TIFFipedia

To become a global leader in the understanding of film, TIFF needs to play a role in documenting Canadian and global film history.

TIFF can host a camp or challenge that taps into the arts communities to help complete entries for Wikipedia, which lacks content in Canadian film entries.

# TORONTO STAR

## Turning drug discovery on its head

DON TAPSCOTT AND RUTH ROSS, TORONTO, ON,
7 MAY 2016: IN.5

Scientists are deciphering the inner workings of the healthy and not-so-healthy brain in fascinating new ways.

With tools like high-volume genome sequencing, synthetic biology, precision imaging, and nanotechnology, research can move forward infinitely faster than was possible even just a few years ago. But considering this progress, why are the 1.5 billion people around the world who live with mental health and brain disorders still left with little more than old-school solutions?

One reason is a research funding and academic system that places a greater value on individual competitiveness over collective brainpower. Individual scientists still compete for narrowly focused grant funding and high-profile journal space, all too often conducting research in relative isolation. In the private sector, a similar model is at play with pharmaceutical companies keeping their R&D secret, leading to the duplication of unshared data.

We are hindered by a century-old model that falls short when it comes to pioneering new and better treatments.

This is all about to change. It has to. For one, pharmaceutical companies have largely pulled out of early-stage R&D, especially in the complex and challenging area of brain research. This leaves a void for visionary, long-term-focused investors to fill—a "demand pull." At the same time, the digital revolution is connecting minds and data across global networks of scientists to enable mass collaboration. Top this "technology push" off with a "demographic kick"—a new generation of young researchers and scientists who have come of age as digital natives—and you have all the ingredients for a drastic realignment.

We are already seeing these forces come together in other areas of biomedical research, with ambitious collaborations like the Structural Genomics Consortium. Based at the University of Toronto, the University of Oxford, and Sweden's Karolinska Institute, this is a not-for-profit, public-private partnership doing the early fundamental science that could lead to new drug discoveries. Researchers collaborate with pharmaceutical company partners on projects such as studying "rogue" cancer-causing proteins and designing chemical probes to identify potential drug targets. The new compounds and discoveries coming out of this work are available free to all other researchers worldwide.

This open-access science speeds up early-stage drug discovery, bypassing lengthy patent and legal agreements and risk analyses. Instead of building fences around their early findings, pioneering firms and researchers are beginning to treat intellectual property more like a mutual fund: they manage a balanced portfolio of intellectual property assets, some protected and some shared. And it's often private donors who are enabling some of the most innovative models—collaborations such as the Donnelly Centre for Cellular and Biomolecular Research, the Ted Rogers Centre for Heart Research, and Medicine by Design.

So could a similar, open-innovation model unlock the potential of neuroscience to yield new treatments in conditions like Alzheimer's disease and mood disorders? Just as we've learned about the brain's remarkable abilities to rewire itself, we think the system of brain research has that same potential.

This is why the University of Toronto is forming a new collaborative model called the Neuroscience Catalyst.

A partnership between academics, research hospitals, and health centres, as well as pharmaceutical company Janssen Inc., it uses the Toronto research community's well-established strengths in brain science to identify the most promising early-stage discoveries and technologies through an open-innovation model.

We are also actively involved in the Psychiatric Genomics Consortium, a federation of more than 200 scientists at 60 institutions in 19 countries committed to sharing data. Researchers from Toronto's Centre for Addiction and Mental Health have helped to identify more than 100 locations in the human genome associated with the risk of developing schizophrenia, in what is the largest genomic study published on any psychiatric disorder to date. By taking down the fence around once-proprietary raw material, we are accelerating the development of new therapies for a disorder that has seen few new treatment options over the past 60 years.

This seismic shift toward collaboration is changing how we work as scientists. Soon the silos in research will be gone—both within universities and between industry and academia.

In their place, collaborative and effective partnerships of the best minds, funded by public as well as private sources, will lead to robust new therapies for the body and for the brain.

# TORONTO STAR

## Universities must change old school of thought

DON TAPSCOTT, TORONTO, ON, 7 MAY 2016: A.26

If there is one institution due for innovation, it's the university. It's time for a deep debate on how universities function in a networked society. The centuries-old model of learning still offered by many big universities doesn't work anymore, especially for students who have grown up digital.

To start with, big universities are still offering what I call the broadcast model of learning, where the teacher is the broadcaster and the student is the supposedly willing recipient of the one-way message. It goes like this: "I'm a professor and I have knowledge. Get ready; here it comes. Your goal is to take this data into your short-term memory so you can recall it to me when I test you."

The definition of a lecture has become the process in which the notes of the teacher go to the notes of the student without going through the brains of either.

This is no longer appropriate for the digital age and for a new generation of students who represent the future of learning. Today's generation wants to converse when they learn. They like to share. Immersed in digital technology, they are keen to try new things, often at high speed. To them, university should be fun and interesting, so they should enjoy the delight of discovering things for themselves.

It's true universities are trying to update this broadcast model. And many professors are working hard to move beyond this model. However, it remains dominant overall.

If universities want to adapt the teaching techniques to their current audience, they should make significant changes, especially if they want to survive the arrival of free online courses, some from the world's top professors.

The professors who remain relevant will have to abandon the traditional lecture and start listening and conversing with the students. To begin, the mastery of knowledge (anything where there is a right or wrong answer) should be achieved by students working with interactive, self-paced computer learning programs. This can be done outside the classroom, freeing students and faculty alike to spend class time on the things that matter: discussion, debate, and collaboration around projects.

This is now possible because of the wonders of modern technology. It is starting to happen at select campuses where professors have introduced a "just in time" approach to their teaching.

Warm-up questions, written by the students, are typically due a few hours before class, giving the teacher an opportunity to adjust the lesson to focus on the parts of the assignments that students struggled with.

Harvard professor Eric Mazur, who uses this approach in his physics class, puts it this way: "Education is so much more than the mere transfer of information. The information has to be assimilated.

Students have to connect the information to what they already know, develop mental models, learn how to apply the new knowledge and how to adapt this knowledge to new and unfamiliar situations."

He's right. What counts these days is your capacity to learn lifelong, to think, research, find information, analyze, synthesize, contextualize, critically evaluate it, to apply research to solving problems, to collaborate and communicate. This is, by the way, what you get out of a liberal arts undergraduate education, no matter which discipline you choose.

Another fixture of old-style learning is the assumption that students should learn on their own. Sharing notes in an exam hall or collaborating on some of the essays and homework assignments was often forbidden. Yet the individual learning model is foreign territory for most young people, who have grown up collaborating, sharing, and creating together online. Progressive educators are recognizing this. Students start internalizing what they've learned in class only once they start talking to each other.

Of course, universities play an important role in the sorting of individuals in society, through the admissions process and the awarding of degrees. They screen human capital for future employers and more broadly stratify society. Those who graduate have the credential to get the most desirable jobs or entrance to graduate programs. They have proven they have a degree of discipline and that they're prepared to play by the rules.

But a credential and even the prestige of a university is rooted in its effectiveness as a learning institution. If campuses are seen as places where learning is inferior to other models or, worse, places where learning is restricted and stifled, the role of the campus experience will be undermined as well. The university is too costly to be simply an extended summer camp. Campuses that embrace the new models become more effective learning environments and more desirable places.

Computer-based learning, for instance, can free up intellectual capital—on the part of both professors and students—to spend their on-campus time thinking and inquiring and challenging each other, rather than just absorbing information.

The current model of university education raises many other questions: Why should a university student be restricted to learning from the professors at the university he or she is attending? True, students can obviously learn from intellectuals around the world through books or the Internet. Yet in a digital world, why shouldn't a student be able to take a course from a professor at another university?

Why are universities judged by the number of students they exclude or by how much they spend? Why aren't they judged by how well they teach and at what price?

The digital world is challenging the very notion of a walled-in institution that excludes large numbers of people. Yet the industrial-age model of education is hard to change. Vested interests fight change. And leaders of old paradigms are often the last to embrace the new.

Back in 1997, I presented my views to a group of about 100 university presidents at a dinner hosted by Ameritech in Chicago. After the talk I sat down at my table and asked the smaller group what they thought about my remarks. They responded positively. So I asked them, "Why is this taking so long?" One president commented that we're still stuck in a "Gutenberg approach to learning."

A very thoughtful man named Jeffery Bannister, then president of Butler College, was seated next to me. "We've got a bunch of professors reading from handwritten notes, writing on blackboards, and the students are writing down what they say," he said.

"This is a not a Gutenberg model. It's a pre-Gutenberg approach—the printing press is not even an important part of the learning paradigm. Wait till these students who are 14 and have grown up learning on the Net hit the (college) classrooms—sparks are going to fly."

Bannister was right. A powerful force to change the university is the students. And sparks are flying today. There is a huge generational clash emerging in these institutions.

Changing the model of pedagogy for this generation is crucial for the survival of the university. If students turn away from a traditional university education, this will erode the value of the credentials universities award, their position as centres of learning and research and as campuses where young people get a chance to grow up.

# THE AUSTRALIAN

## One of the world's most influential management thinkers on how the modern firm is changing

DON TAPSCOTT, AUSTRALIA, 17 JUNE 2016

**You have said that the modern corporation is in the midst of a perfect storm. Please explain.**

Four drivers are transforming the modern firm as we know it. The first is a new paradigm in technology that includes the social web, Big Data, the Internet of Things, cloud computing, robotics, machine learning, and mobility. The next stage of the Internet will be based on the underlying technology of Bitcoin. The blockchain is a globally distributed database of potentially all structured information, and it holds profound implications for the architecture of the corporation and how we create goods and services.

The second change is demographic—but it's not about the ageing population. It's about the young generation of digital natives who have now entered the workforce, bringing with them a new culture of innovation, speed, customization, freedom, integrity, and collaboration.

There is no more powerful force out there to change most of what we know about talent and talent management.

The third driver is economic, and it has to do with the continuing struggles of the global economy as the industrial age comes to an end. For the first time in modern history, the 51st percentile of individuals and families is not getting ahead.

Throughout decades of economic change, wars, even depressions, this group has always managed to progress; but that is not happening today. There are big issues on the table about how to compete through innovation, and create prosperity for everyone.

The fourth driver is the arrival of new business models. Digital conglomerates such as Alphabet, Amazon, and Apple are rapidly evolving into adjacent and not-so-adjacent industries; then there are "data frackers" like Facebook and Dataminr that do "horizontal mining" for data. We're seeing the first wave of service aggregators like Uber and Airbnb. These [new models] are shaking the windows and rattling the doors of traditional business; and through blockchain technology, they are about to be disrupted as well. When you put all of this together, "perfect storm" is probably an understatement for what business leaders are facing.

## You believe that the problems the world faces can be addressed effectively, but we are using the wrong model.

There is no doubt that the world is a very troubled place: it is too unsustainable, unequal, conflicted, and unjust. Poverty in the developed world has gone from $1 (US) ($1.40 Cdn) a day to $2 (US) a day.

Yet half of the world's population is still living on under $10 (US) a day. With problems like conflict, it's hard to say whether it's getting better, and some problems are definitely getting worse. Climate change, for instance, has begun to take some significant tolls.

For the last few decades, the way we have approached these problems is through nation-states, working together in global institutions. This approach began seriously at Bretton Woods in 1944, toward the end of World War II, when we created the World Bank and the International Monetary Fund. A year later, a broader group created the United Nations and then UNESCO, the GATT, the World Trade Organization, the G20, and the G8.

The trouble is, collaboration among nation-states, while still necessary, is now insufficient. Since Bretton Woods, there have been some profound changes: the rise of the corporation; the emergence of a civil society, which didn't really exist in 1944; and the Internet, which dramatically drops transaction and collaboration costs on a global basis. These changes have enabled a new model to emerge: multi-stakeholder networks—or, as my colleagues and I call them, global solutions networks or GSNs.

In some cases, GSNs can govern resources on behalf of the planet. The Internet is governed by a rag-tag ecosystem of global solution networks rather than by nation-states. If we can govern the Internet in this way, what else can we govern? The climate? Perhaps.

## You have identified 10 distinct types of GSNs. Which type is having the most impact thus far?

The most interesting one to me is the governance network, which involves companies, governments at all levels, civil society organizations, NGOs, foundations, academics, and other individuals, co-operating to solve global problems. These combine a series of other GSNs like knowledge networks, advocacy networks, platforms, policy networks, diasporas, watchdog networks, networked institutions, and standards networks.

Old-growth forests are now being governed through such a multi-stakeholder network, and the problem of conflict diamonds is also being managed in this way. These networks are attacking problems like child pornography and child predators on the Internet—issues that cannot be addressed within the context of a nation-state. By far the most exciting thing to me is that we are seeing the emergence of a governance network that could actually govern the world's climate.

## Please describe some of the changes blockchain will bring.

What if there were a next generation of the Internet, where we could conduct peer-to-peer transactions—not just to exchange information, but to exchange value and money? We can't do that today without a powerful intermediary, like a credit card company or PayPal. If we could create commerce without powerful intermediaries, there would be unlimited potential for creating a more prosperous and just world.

Today, 70 per cent of people who own a small piece of land have tenuous rights to that land. Over time, all land registry could be placed on the blockchain, this distributed database of all structured information that is incorruptible and unhackable. That way, no dictator could say, "You don't own this land; my friend does."

What if half a trillion dollars in remittance from the world's diasporas didn't go into transaction fees, but was actually sent to the people who needed the money? What if we could create companies with tens of millions of shareholders by holding Kickstarter-like campaigns on the blockchain? What if musicians, rather than receiving crumbs for the value they create, got fed first by posting their music with associated rights and contracts on the blockchain? Those are just a few of dozens of examples.

### Given all of the above, are you optimistic about the future?

I am, because of the coming blockchain revolution. As indicated, the first era of the digital age has not fully delivered on its promise.

We now have another opportunity to rewrite the economic order of things and dramatically improve the state of the world.

### What skills are required to lead today?

The person at the top cannot learn for the organization as a whole any more. Things have become too complicated, and leadership must, as Peter Senge said, become "leadership for learning." It is now possible—and important—for people throughout an organization to behave as leaders. The new collaborative systems that are being designed actually call for this. Talent and leadership from anywhere in your organization—and even from outside of it—must be harnessed.

# HARVARD BUSINESS REVIEW

## How blockchain is changing finance

ALEX TAPSCOTT AND DON TAPSCOTT, 1 MARCH 2017

Our global financial system moves trillions of dollars a day and serves billions of people. But the system is rife with problems, adding cost through fees and delays, creating friction through redundant and onerous paperwork, and opening up opportunities for fraud and crime. To wit, 45 per cent of financial intermediaries, such as payment networks, stock exchanges, and money transfer services, suffer from economic crime every year; the number is 37 per cent for the entire economy, and only 20 per cent and 27 per cent for the professional services and technology sectors, respectively. It's no small wonder that regulatory costs continue to climb and remain a top concern for bankers. This all adds cost, with consumers ultimately bearing the burden.

It leads to the question: Why is our financial system so inefficient? First, because it's antiquated, a kludge of industrial technologies and paper-based processes dressed up in a digital wrapper. Second, because it's centralized, which makes it resistant to change and vulnerable to systems failures and attacks. Third, it's exclusionary, denying billions of people access to basic financial tools. Bankers have largely dodged the sort of creative destruction that, while messy, is critical to economic vitality and progress. But the solution to this innovation logjam has emerged: blockchain.

# How blockchain works

Here are five basic principles underlying the technology.

## 1. Distributed database

Each party on a blockchain has access to the entire database and its complete history. No single party controls the data or the information. Every party can verify the records of its transaction partners directly, without an intermediary.

## 2. Peer-to-peer transmission

Communication occurs directly between peers instead of through a central node. Each node stores and forwards information to all other nodes.

## 3. Transparency with pseudonymity

Every transaction and its associated value are visible to anyone with access to the system. Each node, or user, on a blockchain has a unique 30-plus-character alphanumeric address that identifies it. Users can choose to remain anonymous or provide proof of their identity to others. Transactions occur between blockchain addresses.

## 4. Irreversibility of records

Once a transaction is entered in the database and the accounts are updated, the records cannot be altered, because they're linked to every transaction record that came before them (hence the term "chain"). Various computational algorithms and approaches are deployed to ensure that the recording on the database is permanent, chronologically ordered, and available to all others on the network.

## 5. Computational logic

The digital nature of the ledger means that blockchain transactions can be tied to computational logic and in essence programmed. So users can set up algorithms and rules that automatically trigger transactions between nodes. Blockchain was originally developed as the technology behind cryptocurrencies like Bitcoin. A vast, globally distributed ledger running on millions of devices, it is capable of recording anything of value. Money, equities, bonds, titles, deeds, contracts, and virtually all other kinds of assets can be moved and stored securely, privately, and from peer to peer, because trust is established not by powerful intermediaries like banks and governments, but by network consensus, cryptography, collaboration, and clever code. For the first time in human history, two or more parties, be they businesses or individuals who may not even know each other, can forge agreements, make transactions, and build value without relying on intermediaries (such as banks, rating agencies, and government bodies such as the US Department of State) to verify their identities, establish trust, or perform the critical business logic—contracting, clearing, settling, and record-keeping tasks that are foundational to all forms of commerce.

Given the promise and peril of such a disruptive technology, many firms in the financial industry, such as banks, insurers, and audit and professional service firms, are investing in blockchain solutions. What is driving this deluge of money and interest? Most firms cite opportunities to reduce friction and costs. After all, most financial intermediaries themselves rely on a dizzying, complex, and costly array of intermediaries to run their own operations. Santander, a European bank, put the potential savings at $20 billion a year. Capgemini, a consultancy, estimates that consumers could save up to $16 billion in banking and insurance fees each year through block-chain-based applications.

To be sure, blockchain may enable incumbents such as JPMorgan Chase, Citigroup, and Credit Suisse, all of which are currently investing in the technology, to do more with less, streamline their businesses, and reduce risk in the process. But while an opportunistic viewpoint is advantageous and often necessary, it is rarely sufficient. After all, how do you cut cost from a business or market whose structure has fundamentally changed? Here, blockchain is a real game changer. By reducing transaction costs among all participants in the economy, blockchain supports models of peer-to-peer mass collaboration that could make many of our existing organizational forms redundant.

For example, consider how new business ventures access growth capital. Traditionally, companies target angel investors in the early stages of a new business and later look to venture capitalists, eventually culminating in an initial public offering (IPO) on a stock exchange. This industry supports a number of intermediaries, such as investment bankers, exchange operators, auditors, lawyers, and crowdfunding platforms (such as Kickstarter and Indiegogo).

Blockchain changes the equation by enabling companies of any size to raise money in a peer-to-peer way, through global distributed share offerings. This new funding mechanism is already transforming the blockchain industry. In 2016 blockchain companies raised $400 million from traditional venture investors and nearly $200 million through what we call initial coin offerings (ICO rather than IPO). These ICOs aren't just new cryptocurrencies masquerading as companies. They represent content and digital rights management platforms (such as SingularDTV), distributed venture funds (such as the DAO, for decentralized autonomous organization), and even new platforms to make investing in ICOs and managing digital assets easy (such as ICONOMI). There is already a deep pipeline of ICOs this year, such as Cosmos, a unifying technology that will connect every blockchain in the world, which is why it's been dubbed the "Internet of blockchains." Others are sure to follow suit. In 2017 we expect that blockchain startups will raise more funds through ICO than any other means—a historic inflection point.

Incumbents are taking notice. The New York–based venture capital firm Union Square Ventures (USV) broadened its investment strategy so that it could buy ICOs directly. Menlo Park venture capital firm Andreessen Horowitz joined USV in investing in Polychain Capital, a hedge fund that only buys tokens. Blockchain Capital, one of the industry's largest investors, recently announced that it would be raising money for its new fund by issuing tokens by ICO, a first for the industry. And, of course, companies such as Goldman Sachs, NASDAQ, Inc., and Intercontinental Exchange, the American holding company that owns the New York Stock Exchange, which dominate the IPO and listing business, have been among the largest investors in blockchain ventures.

As with any radically new business model, ICOs have risks. There is little to no regulatory oversight. Due diligence and disclosures can be scant, and some companies that have issued ICOs have gone bust. Caveat emptor is the watchword, and many of the early backers are more punters than funders. But the genie has been unleashed from the bottle. Done right, ICOs can not only improve the efficiency of raising money, lowering the cost of capital for entrepreneurs and investors, but also democratize participation in global capital markets.

If the world of venture capital can change radically in one year, what else can we transform? Blockchain could upend a number of complex intermediate functions in the industry: identity and reputation, moving value (payments and remittances), storing value (savings), lending and borrowing (credit), trading value (marketplaces like stock exchanges), insurance and risk management, and audit and tax functions.

Is this the end of banking as we know it? That depends on how incumbents react. Blockchain is not an existential threat to those who embrace the new technology paradigm and disrupt from within. The question is, who in the financial services industry will lead the revolution? Throughout history, leaders of old paradigms have struggled to embrace the new. Why didn't AT&T launch Skype, or Visa create PayPal? CNN could have built Twitter, since it is all about the sound bite. GM or Hertz could have launched Uber; Marriott could have invented Airbnb. The unstoppable force of blockchain technology is barreling down on the infrastructure of modern finance. As with prior paradigm shifts, blockchain will create winners and losers. Personally, we would like the inevitable collision to transform the old money machine into a prosperity platform for all.

# EDUCAUSE REVIEW

## The blockchain revolution and higher education

ALEX TAPSCOTT AND DON TAPSCOTT, MARCH/APRIL 2017

What will be the most important technology to change higher education? In our view, it's not big data, the social web, MOOCs, virtual reality, or even artificial intelligence. We see these as components of something new, all enabled and transformed by an emerging technology called the blockchain. Okay, it's not the most sonorous word ever, sounding more like a college football strategy than a transformative technology. Yet, sonorous or not, the blockchain represents nothing less than the second generation of the Internet, and it holds the potential to disrupt money, business, government, and yes, higher education.

The opportunities for innovators in higher education fall into four categories:

- *Identity and student records:* How we identify students; protect their privacy; measure, record, and credential their accomplishments; and keep these records secure

- *New pedagogy:* How we customize teaching to each student and create new models of learning

- *Costs (student debt):* How we value and fund education and reward students for the quality of their work

- *The meta-university:* How we design entirely new models of higher education so that former MIT president Chuck Vest's dream can become a reality.[1]

The blockchain may help us change the relationships among colleges and universities and, in turn, their relationship to society.
Let us explain.

## What is the blockchain revolution?

The Internet today connects billions of people around the world, and certainly it's great for communicating and collaborating online. But because it's built for moving and storing information rather than value, it has done little to change how we do business. When professors send their students information such as an email, lecture notes, a PowerPoint presentation, or an audio recording of a lecture, they're really sending a copy, not the original. It's okay (and indeed advantageous) for people to print a copy of their PowerPoint file, but it's not okay to print, say, money or diplomas. So with the Internet of information, we have to rely on powerful intermediaries to exchange things of value. Governments, banks, digital platforms (e.g., Amazon, eBay, and Airbnb), and colleges and universities do the work of establishing our identity, vouching for our trustworthiness, and helping us to acquire and transfer assets and settle the transactions.

Overall, they do a pretty good job—but there are limitations. They use centralized servers, which can be hacked. They take a piece of the value for performing this service—say, 10 per cent to send some money internationally. They capture our data, not just preventing us from using it for our own benefit but often undermining our privacy. These intermediaries are sometimes unreliable and often slow. They exclude two billion people who don't have enough money to justify a bank account, let alone an education. Most problematic, they are capturing the benefits of the digital age asymmetrically. What if there was an Internet of value—a global, distributed, highly secure platform, ledger, or database where we could store and exchange things of value and where we could trust each other without powerful intermediaries? That is the blockchain. Collective self-interest, hard-coded into this new native digital medium for value, would ensure the safety, security, and reliability of our exchanges online. Trust is programmed into the technology, which is why we call blockchain the Trust Protocol.

Why should you care? Maybe you're a music professor who wants artists to make a living off their art. Perhaps you're an immigrant who is sick of paying big fees to send money home so that your children can go to college in your ancestral land. Or maybe you're a parent fed up with the lack of transparency and accountability of the politicians and political appointees responsible for higher education in your state. Or perhaps you're a social media user who thinks all the data you generate might be worth something—to you—and that your privacy matters. Even as we write, innovators are building blockchain-based applications that serve these ends. And these apps are just the beginning.

It turns out that every business, institution, government, and individual can benefit in profound ways. How about the corporation, a pillar of modern capitalism? With the rise of a global peer-to-peer platform for identity, trust, reputation, and transactions, we will be able to reengineer deep structures of the firm, for innovation and shared value creation. We're talking about building 21st-century companies that look more like networks than the vertically integrated hierarchies of the industrial age. The whole financial services industry is already being reinvented by the blockchain, and others will soon follow. How well does today's college or university prepare students for such a future?

How about the Internet of Things? In the not-too-distant future, billions of smart things in the physical world will be sensing, responding, communicating, sharing important data, and generating, buying, and selling their own electricity, doing everything from protecting our environment to managing our health. It turns out that this Internet of Everything will need a *Ledger of Everything*.

One of the biggest opportunities of the blockchain is to free us from the grip of a troubling prosperity paradox. The economy is growing, but fewer people are benefiting. Rather than trying to solve the problem of growing social inequality through redistribution alone, we can change how wealth—and opportunity—is predistributed in the first place, as people everywhere, from farmers to musicians, can use this technology to share more fully in the wealth they create.

## Blockchain, identity, and student records

"Today you need an organization with endowed rights to provide you with an identity," said Carlos Moreira of WISeKey.[2] This process of identification usually begins with a birth certificate issued by a state-licensed medical professional. From that day forward, the baby begins to accumulate personal data, which will include academic achievements in analog form.

The first challenge is to maintain the privacy and security of data stored digitally by those academically accredited institutions. In 2013, the Education Advisory Board (EAB) published a list of 157 strategies for collecting data about students and alumni for colleges and universities to exploit in fundraising efforts, and institutions have become good at doing so.[3] When it comes to protecting these data, however, colleges and universities are no less vulnerable than other large organizations. The University of California–Berkeley, Ohio State University, the University of Wisconsin–Milwaukee, and Kirkwood Community College were among those hacked in recent years. Yale University accidentally published confidential information online, and Indiana University hosted such data on an unprotected site. The University of Utah Hospitals and Clinics, Stanford University, and the University of Miami stored data on laptops or data tapes that were later stolen.[4]

The blockchain can be programmed to record virtually everything of value and importance to humankind, starting with birth certificates and moving on to educational transcripts, social security cards, student loans, and anything else that can be expressed in code. The blockchain uses public key infrastructure (PKI) for establishing a secure platform.

PKI is an advanced form of asymmetric cryptography, where users get two keys that don't perform the same function: one is for encryption and the other for decryption. Hence, they are asymmetric. The Bitcoin blockchain is now the largest civilian deployment of PKI in the world, second overall to the US Department of Defense common access system.[5] Sony Global Education has adapted this technology into what it is calling an open data exchange protocol, through which two parties anywhere in the world can securely share official academic records.[6] But without the exact two keys, a hacker cannot access the data.

A second challenge to address is validity. At a time when information is abundant, fleeting, and mutable, being able to verify a job prospect's claims is becoming increasingly important to employers. According to CareerBuilder, 57 per cent of job applicants have embellished their skill set, and 33 per cent have lied about their academic degree.[7] Not surprisingly, employers are wanting to see official college transcripts. However, when it comes to processing requests, universities often charge transaction fees. At MIT, for example, "the base cost for a transcript is $8.00" with a $2.00 handling charge for each transcript ordered online.[8] Sony's solution could make the transfer of such information quick and comparatively cost-free. Imagine how such a system could benefit, say, refugees who were seeking to continue their education or find a job in a new country.

A third issue is time. In the United States, only 25 per cent of students attend college full-time at residential campuses. The rest are juggling work and family. These part-time students take twice as long to graduate, and only 25 per cent of them actually earn a degree.[9] Initiatives such as OpenBadges, Blockchain Certificates, and Learning Is Earning 2026 are exploring ways to reward students with credentials for everything they learn, no matter the setting. If a parent teaches his or her child how to change the oil in a car, that counts (and the parent gets teaching credit). If a student learns a new skill at work, or has to collaborate to finish a task, or is managing others, that goes on the learning transcript too. The MIT Media Lab started hashing digital certificates onto the blockchain to permanently denote membership and to reward community members for their valuable contributions to the lab's work.[10] Students are not getting just a grade; they are getting a credential, which they can put to use immediately on the job market.

## Blockchain and the new pedagogy

As long as society—or at least today's employers, including governments—values existing credentials, and students will pay to get those credentials at recognized institutions of higher education rather than pursue alternatives, then the college/university will remain a gatekeeper to opportunity.

But the credential and even the prestige of a higher education institution are rooted in its effectiveness as a learning institution. If colleges and universities become seen as places where learning is inferior to other models or, worse, as places where learning is restricted and stifled, then the role of the campus experience and the credential itself will be undermined. Attending a college or university is too costly to be simply an extended summer camp. Campuses that embrace the new models become more effective learning environments and more desirable places. Computer-based learning, for instance, can free up intellectual capital—on the part of both professors and students—to spend their on-campus time thinking, inquiring, and challenging each other, rather than just absorbing information.

If there is one thing that's due for innovation in higher education, it's the model of pedagogy. To start with, big universities are still offering the broadcast model of learning, in which the teacher is the broadcaster and the student is the supposedly willing recipient of the one-way message. It goes like this: "I'm a professor, and I have knowledge. Get ready; here it comes. Your goal is to take this data into your short-term memory so that you can recall it to me when I test you."

The definition of a lecture has become the process in which the notes of the teacher go to the notes of the student without going through the brains of either. This is no longer appropriate for the digital age and for a new generation of students who represent the future of learning. Young people want to converse when they learn. They like to share. Immersed in digital technology, they are keen to try new things, often at high speed. They want their education to be fun and interesting. So they should enjoy the delight of discovering things for themselves.

It's true that colleges and universities are trying to update this broadcast model—through essays, hands-on labs, and even seminar discussions. And of course, many professors are working hard to move beyond this model. However, it remains dominant overall. The professors who remain relevant will have to abandon the traditional lecture and start listening to and conversing with the students. To begin, students could achieve the mastery of knowledge (anything where there is a right or wrong answer) by working with interactive, self-paced computer learning programs outside the classroom, freeing students and faculty alike to spend class time on the things that matter: discussion, debate, and collaboration around projects.

We also need to be clear on the purpose of higher education. It's not about skills, and to a certain extent, it's not even about knowledge.

What counts these days is the capacity to learn throughout life; to research, analyze, synthesize, contextualize, and critically evaluate information; to apply research in solving problems; and to collaborate and communicate.

So how can blockchains help? Consider the case of Vitalik Buterin, the founder of the Ethereum blockchain. Like many teenagers, Buterin "spent ridiculous amounts of time on the Internet," reading about different ideas that were heterodox, out of the mainstream.[11] Ask him which economists he likes, and he rattles off Tyler Cowen, Alex Tabarrok, Robin Hanson, and Bryan Caplan. He can speak on the works of the game theorist Thomas Schelling and the behavioural economists Daniel Kahneman and Dan Ariely. "It's actually surprisingly useful how much you can learn for yourself by debating ideas like politics with other people on forums. It's a surprising educational experience all by itself," he said. The topic of Bitcoin, he noted, kept coming up.

"I had all these different interests, and somehow Bitcoin seemed like a perfect convergence. It has this math. It has its computer science. It has its cryptography. It has its economics. It has its political and social philosophy. It was this community that I was immediately drawn into," he said. "I found it really empowering." He went through the online forums, looked for ways to own some Bitcoin and discovered a guy who was starting up a Bitcoin blog. "It was called *Bitcoin Weekly*, and he was offering people five Bitcoins to write articles for him. That was around four dollars at the time," Buterin said. "I wrote a few articles. I earned 20 Bitcoins. I spent half of them on a T-shirt. Going through that whole process, it felt almost like working with the fundamental building blocks of society." How many students have that experience in college?

By the end of that year, Buterin was spending 10 to 20 hours a week writing for another publication, *Bitcoin Magazine*. "When I was about eight months into university, I realized that it had taken over my entire life, and I might as well let it take over my entire life. Waterloo was a really good university and I really liked the program. My dropping out was definitely not a case of the university sucking. It was more a matter of 'That was fun, and this is more fun.' It was a once-in-a-lifetime opportunity, and I just basically couldn't let it go." He was only 17 years old.

Buterin is a natural-born leader, in that he pulls people along with his ideas and his vision. Shouldn't the university experience cultivate these assets rather than get in the way of them?

In 2011, the technology entrepreneur and investor Peter Thiel launched his two-year fellowship program for "young people who want to build new things." Thiel's target audience consists of students who "skip or [drop] out of college to receive a $100,000 grant and support from the Thiel Foundation's network of founders, investors, and scientists." The approach is similar to Buterin's: students learn by working on something they care about, such as clean water. Thus far, Thiel Fellows have started more than 60 companies with a combined value of $1.1 billion. Blockchains provide a platform for such collaboration, not just tracking people's individual contributions but also rewarding them for results.

A good model for classroom collaboration is Consensus Systems (ConsenSys), one of the first Ethereum software-development companies. It is breaking new ground in management science along the lines of holacracy, a collaborative rather than hierarchical process for defining and aligning the work to be done. Among those holacratic tenets are "dynamic roles rather than traditional job descriptions; distributed, not delegated authority; transparent rules rather than office politics; and rapid reiterations rather than big reorganizations," all of which describe how blockchain technologies work.[12] How ConsenSys is structured, how it creates value, and how it manages itself differs not only from the typical classroom but also from the typical online course.

For the most part, members of ConsenSys choose two to five projects to work on. No top-down assignments. There is no boss. Everyone owns a piece of every project directly or indirectly: the Ethereum platform issues tokens that members can exchange for Ether and then convert into any other currency. The goal is to achieve a balance between independence and interdependence. For the classroom, the watchwords are *agility*, *openness*, and *consensus*: identify what needs to be learned; distribute the load among the students eager and able to do it; agree on their roles, responsibilities, and rewards; and then codify these rights in smart contracts. Teachers and students alike would need training to participate in such a system.

### How Blockchains Establish Trust

Digital assets—everything from money, stocks, bonds, and intellectual property to loyalty points and student records—are not all stored in a central place: they're distributed across a global ledger, using the highest level of cryptography. When a transaction is conducted, it's posted globally, across millions of computers. Around the world is a group of people called miners who have massive computing power at their fingertips—10 to 100 times bigger than all of Google worldwide. Every 10 minutes, kind of like the heartbeat of a network, these miners assemble all the transactions from the previous 10 minutes into a block. Then the miners compete to solve a tough problem; whoever solves the problem gets to validate the block and receives some digital currency as a reward. In the case of the Bitcoin blockchain, the winner gets Bitcoin.

Then that block is linked to the previous block and to the block before that to create a chain of blocks. Every block is time-stamped, kind of like with a digital waxed seal. So if you wanted to hack a block and, say, send the same Bitcoin to several people, you'd have to hack that block, plus all the preceding blocks, through the entire history of that Bitcoin on the blockchain—not just on one computer but across millions of computers, simultaneously, all using the highest levels of encryption, in broad daylight. Tough to do. This is infinitely more secure than the computer systems that we use today.

The Bitcoin blockchain is just one of many. For example, the Ethereum blockchain was developed by a 22-year-old Canadian named Vitalik Buterin. Ethereum has some extraordinary capabilities and tools. For example, it enables programmers to build smart contracts, agreements translated into lines of computer code that handle the enforcement, management, performance, and payments of contracts between people. On the Ethereum blockchain, there are projects to create a replacement for the stock market and a new model of democracy, where politicians are accountable to citizens.

## Blockchain and costs (student debt)

Many educators have a problem with the idea of education as big business, and yet companies like Pearson and McGraw-Hill make their fortunes by providing the classroom content, additional teacher training, classroom and school administration systems, and the testing content and platforms—the results of which lead to credentials, not just of high school diplomas and college entrance but of individual licensures and professional certifications. These companies have considerable budgets for lobbying federal and state legislators.

Let's look at the numbers. From 1995 to 2015, the average tuition and fees at private colleges and universities increased 179 per cent. Tuition and fees for out-of-state students at public universities jumped 226 per cent, and in-state tuition and fees ballooned by 296 per cent.[13] Approximately 44 million Americans owe a grand total of $1.3 trillion in student loans. A member of the Class of 2016 racked up, on average, $37,172 in debt.[14] It's no wonder that cost of a college education was such a hot issue in the 2016 US presidential election.

Melanie Swan is looking to the blockchain to tackle student debt head-on. She is the founder of the Institute for Blockchain Studies. She has been working on MOOC accreditation and "pay for success" models on the blockchain. The blockchain provides three elements toward this goal: (1) a trustable proof-of-truth mechanism to confirm that the students who signed up for Coursera classes actually completed them, took the tests, and mastered the material; (2) a payment mechanism; and (3) smart contracts that could constitute learning plans.

Consider smart contracts for coding skills. "Why don't we target financial aid toward personal development?" Swan said.[15] It works like the micro-funding organization Kiva, but Kiva for coding classes rather than for entrepreneurial startups; everything would be super transparent, and students would be accountable for their progress.

Donors—such as companies that need specific skills—could sponsor individual students, put money toward learning goals, and pay out according to achievement. Let's say you wanted to support a female student who lives in Nigeria and is going through Google's Training for Android developers. Every week this student would need to provide proof of completion of a development module. Perhaps this is all automated through an online test where the blockchain confirms the student's identity and records progress[16] before disbursing the next week's funding— into what we could call the student's "smart wallet for higher education"—so that the student could continue paying for college courses without interference. This could all be accomplished without a not-for-profit or government agency with administrative costs and the power to change funding. "Money toward a girl's education couldn't be diverted to her brother's schooling," Swan said.

The visionaries behind the Learning Is Earning initiative, such as Jane McGonigal, in partnership with the Institute for the Future and the ACT Foundation, envision "teach it forward" schemes in which students can pay down their student loans by teaching other students what they just learned or by applying this new knowledge immediately in the job market.[17] They needn't wait for a degree to begin earning money. Employers—or other students or professors— will be able to query the blockchain for people with the particular combination of skills and knowledge needed immediately on the job or in the classroom. In other words, the blockchain will help employers match projects with the proven capabilities of students available for project work. Students will be able to link these earnings with a particular lecture or skill so that they can calculate the precise value of each element of their training and development. Likewise, human resources personnel will be able to calculate the return on their training and development investments. Employers may even be willing to pay for a student's entire education in exchange for a cut of the student's future earnings. Academic publishers may be willing to pay for some of this tracking data to improve their learning modules for all types of learners, since they won't have access to it otherwise on the blockchain.[18]

## The blockchain and the meta-university

The term *ivory tower* usually carries pejorative connotations. From the 19th century, it has been used to designate a world or atmosphere in which intellectuals engage in pursuits that are disconnected from the practical concerns of everyday life. For cynics, it connotes a wilful separation from the everyday world; esoteric, overspecialized, or even useless research; and academic elitism, if not outright condescension. If we set aside some of these more negative associations, the ivory tower metaphor still captures one of the key flaws in today's system of higher learning: in a world of unprecedented connectivity, especially among today's youth, colleges and universities continue to operate as largely autonomous islands of scholarship and learning and have thus far failed to use the Internet to break down the walls that divide institutions, professors, parents, and students.

The blockchain will enable the 21st-century institution of higher education to disaggregate into a network and an ecosystem—not a tower. Indeed, innovators have an enormous opportunity to create an unparalleled educational experience for students globally by assembling the world's best learning materials online and enabling students to customize their learning path with support from a network of instructors and educational facilitators, some of whom may be local and some halfway around the globe. To make this work for students, colleges and universities will require deep structural changes, and educators will need to embrace the partnerships. In 2006, MIT president emeritus Charles Vest offered a tantalizing vision of what he called the meta-university. In the open-access movement, he saw "a transcendent, accessible, empowering, dynamic, communally constructed framework of open materials and platforms on which much of higher education worldwide can be constructed or enhanced."[19] The web would provide the communication infrastructure, and a global open-access library of course materials would provide much of the knowledge and information infrastructure. Dr. Vest argued that a noble and global endeavour of this scale would speed the propagation of high-quality education and give teachers and students everywhere the ability to access and share teaching materials, scholarly publications, and scientific works in progress and to participate in real-time science experiments.

However, without a means of associating students' identities with their achievements, recording and credentialling these achievements over time, rewarding constructive and collaborative behaviour in the community, and otherwise holding participants accountable for deliverables, this Internet-only meta-university would still fall short of traditional education. An average of only 15 per cent of students who sign up for MOOCs complete them; free MOOCs are still considered supplemental to tuition-based online courses from traditional colleges and universities.[20]

The blockchain provides a rich, secure, and transparent platform on which to create such a global network for higher learning.[21] We envision three stages. The first is content exchange. Professors share ideas and upload their teaching materials to the Internet for others to use freely. The second is content co-innovation, where teachers collaborate across institutional and disciplinary boundaries to co-create new teaching materials using wikis and other tools. By stage three, the college or university has become a node in the global network of faculty, students, and institutions learning collaboratively. It still maintains its identity, campus, and brand. The global network for higher learning is not a pipe dream. Leading scholars know that higher education institutions and their faculties cannot continue to operate as islands, constantly reinventing the lecture.

## Stage 1: Content exchange

The lowest level of collaborative knowledge production is simple content exchange: colleges and universities post their educational materials online, putting into the public domain what would have traditionally been considered a proprietary asset and part of the institution's competitive advantage in the global market for students. MIT pioneered the concept, and today more than 200 institutions of higher learning have followed suit as part of MIT's OpenCourseWare initiative. OpenCourseWare solves the problem of isolation and provides a wealth of materials that others can use and even build on, regardless of their institutional affiliation. We're talking about not only textbooks and digital books but also lecture notes, assignments, exams, videos, podcasts, and so on. Professors and students will need better tools for gauging the quality and suitability of various assets, and students will want some evidence of effort to carry forward. Using capabilities like smart contracts, blockchains provide a means of tracking and rewarding each party's contributions. Users can do more than "like," "upvote," or share a piece of content; they can send its creator some tokens of value that might be used, say, to support research assistance or grant writing. Members of the worldwide academic community will have incentive to contribute their intellectual property, know-how, and insights not just to improve higher education but also to enhance their own reputations and even to receive material or financial benefit. Newcomers will be able to see not only the most used content relevant to their studies but also the most valued contributors. For-profit academic journal and textbook publishers can participate in, rather than intermediate, value creation.

## Stage 2: Content co-innovation

The next level in collaborative knowledge creation goes beyond discussing and sharing ideas to the actual co-creation of content. Just as Wikipedia's distributed editors collaborate to create, update, and expand the online encyclopedia's entries, so too could professors co-innovate new teaching material, publish this newly synthesized content, and share in the recognition and rewards.

A case in point is Wikiversity, a project of the Wikimedia Foundation. Rather than offer a set menu of courses and materials, Wikiversity participants set out what they want to learn, and the Wikiversity community collaborates, in multiple languages, to develop learning activities and projects to accommodate those goals. Imagine what a platform like Wikiversity could do with a token system to reward collaborative behaviour! That's what the blockchain supports. It enables the community to identify valuable projects, assemble teams of collaborators, and fund each phase of development, rewarding collaborators according to their contributions.

In this scenario, psychology professors would work together to design the "perfect course" that pools the collective knowledge of the world's leading thinkers in the field. Of course, participants would not agree totally on course contents, since there are various perspectives, schools of thought, and teaching techniques. But as in Wikipedia, the professors could work globally to create core, generally agreed-upon modules, and then subnetworks of like-minded teachers could develop ancillary elements. For the ultimate course, the teachers would need more than course materials—they would need course software allowing students to interact with the content, supporting small-group discussions, enabling testing and scoring, and issuing badges for completion.

If thousands of people can develop Linux, the most sophisticated computer operating system in the world, they can certainly develop the tools for a psychology course. Indeed, many well-known open-source software projects are already underway in the academic community. One of the most popular is Sakai. Built by educators for educators, Sakai facilitates collaboration in and across courses, research, projects, administrative processes, and multidisciplinary and multi-institution efforts. Creation of the software itself is a product of content co-innovation. In turn, the product helps users co-innovate content that educators can teach to students. We need more projects like this.

Used properly, blockchain platforms could support such collaboration directly with students too. Rather than simply receiving the professor's knowledge, the students could co-create knowledge with light supervision—one of the most effective methods of learning—and get credit for their co-creation.

## Stage 3: Global network

The upshot could be a disaggregation of institutions of higher learning. The digital world, which has trained young minds to inquire and collaborate, is challenging not only the lecture-driven classroom but the very notion of a walled-in institution that excludes large numbers of people. Why not allow a brilliant ninth-grader to take first-year college math, without abandoning the social life of his or her high school? Why use the concept of grades and grade matriculation at all? Why not encourage a foreign student majoring in math to take a high school English course? Why is the college or university the unit of measurement when it comes to branding a degree? In fact, in a networked world, why should students have to assign their "enrolment" to a given institution, akin to declaring loyalty to some feudal fiefdom? In this vision of a global network for higher learning, a student receives a custom learning experience from a dozen institutions, while the blockchain serves to track the student's path and progress. The student enrols in his or her primary college and is assigned a knowledge facilitator, who works with the student to customize a learning experience, the journey, and outcomes. The student might enrol in the primary college in Oregon and register to take a behavioural psychology course from Stanford University and a medieval history course from Cambridge. For these students, the collective syllabi of the world form their menu for higher education. Yet the opportunity goes beyond simply mixing and matching courses. Next-generation faculty will create a context whereby students from around the world can participate in online discussions, forums, and wikis to discover, learn, and produce knowledge as a community of learners who are engaged directly in addressing some of the world's most pressing problems. The blockchain harmonizes and aggregates the records of various institutions for each skill learned and each module completed, steadily building an individual student's list of achievements. Of course, such open platforms could provide a means to address the needs of all learners, not just traditional college-age students. For today's knowledge workers, remaining truly competitive in fast-moving fields of research and innovation means constantly retraining and retooling to begin or continue their working lives in a modern, dynamic, and technology-focused environment. The cost of building new continuing education programs from scratch could be prohibitively high, but innovative models of collaborative education could bring greater efficiency, creativity, and credentialling to lifelong learning initiatives.[22] Indeed, why not allow companies and governments to participate in this global network for higher learning? Platform developers could use fees collected from commercial users to subsidize ongoing development.

## Incentives to change

If all this innovation is a good idea, what are the incentives to change? Why should professors adopt a new model of pedagogy? Tenure continues to prop up the lecture model. The US publishing industry provides much of the classroom curriculum, the administrative and engagement platforms, and the testing programs for credentialling at all levels of academic achievement. So if you're an academic or an administrator, you might say: "Let the publishers rethink the student experience. Why should I bother? I have enough on my plate."

Indeed, there are few incentives to change—except that the new model of higher education is in the best interest of learners. Faculty and administrators alike should consider what has happened to other cultural institutions that have resisted change. Encyclopedias, newspapers, record labels, and colleges/universities have a lot in common. They are all in the business of producing content. They all recruit, manage, and compensate capable producers. They all offer proprietary products, and they take legal action against those who infringe their intellectual property. Because they create unique value, their customers pay them, and they have revenue. All of these businesses are possible because of scarcity—in quality news, information, knowledge, learning, art.

Today, the businesses of encyclopedias, newspapers, and record labels are in various stages of collapse. Because of the Internet, they've lost their monopolies on the creation and curation of quality content. The digital age brought abundance, mass participation, new delivery channels, and new business models. The Internet erased their allegedly unassailable attributes faster than you can transfer Bitcoin from one phone to another. In each sector, only two or three global behemoths remain.

Colleges and universities have not yet lost their monopoly on academic credentialling and educational brands. But again we have a case of an irresistible force (i.e., the reinvention of higher learning) meeting an immovable object (i.e., the old paradigm). As soon as one of the blockchain-based innovators demonstrates that its approach to learning will pay off more quickly, that employers value its credentials as much if not more, and that it can deliver real value to the great many students who cannot afford college tuition or whose cognitive or social abilities don't "fit" traditional pedagogy, then rest assured: students will demand more for their money than what they are receiving from traditional institutions of higher education.

Why not be leaders for a new paradigm? The blockchain provides a rich, secure, and transparent platform on which to create a global network for higher learning. We believe that higher education works best when it works for all types of teaching and learning, and we believe that this new platform is an engine of inclusion. Let's use the emerging Internet of value and the blockchain revolution to recapture our identities and endow them with our detailed and real-time records of learning. Perhaps then we can finally reinvent the past model of pedagogy and transform the architecture of higher education for the future generation of lifelong learners.

# Notes

1.  Charles M. Vest, "Open Content and the Emerging Global Meta-University," *EDUCAUSE Review* 41, no. 3 (May/June 2006).

2.  Carlos Creus Moreira, interview with the authors, September 3, 2015. Moreira is founder, chair, and CEO of WISeKey.

3.  EAB, "Strategies for Alumni and Student Data Collection," September 5, 2013.

4.  "World's Biggest Data Breaches," *Information Is Beautiful* (updated January 5, 2017).

5.  Andreas M. Antonopoulos, interview with the authors, July 20, 2015. Antonopoulos is the author of *Mastering Bitcoin* (2014), The Internet of Money (2016), and with co-author Gavin Wood, *Mastering Ethereum* (2017).

6.  "Sony Global Education Develops Technology Using Blockchain for Open Sharing of Academic Proficiency and Progress Records," news release, February 22, 2016.

7.  "Fifty-Eight Per Cent of Employers Have Caught a Lie on a Resumé, According to a New CareerBuilder Survey," news release, August 7, 2014. See also Charles Purdy, "The Biggest Lies Job Seekers Tell on Their Resumés—and How They Get Caught," Monster, accessed January 24, 2017, and "Resumé Falsification Statistics," Statistic Brain, October 1, 2015.

8.  MIT Registrar's Office, Transcripts, accessed January 8, 2017.

9.  Complete College America, "Time Is the Enemy," September 2011. https://completecollege.org/wp-content/uploads/2017/08/Time_Is_the_Enemy.pdf

10. Philipp Schmidt, "Certificates, Reputation, and the Blockchain," MIT Media Lab, *Medium*, October 27, 2015.

11. These and the following quotes are from Vitalik Buterin, interview with the authors, September 30, 2015.

12. Joseph Lubin, interview with the authors, July 13, 2015. Lubin is the founder and CEO of ConsenSys, an Ethereum development studio.

13. Travis Mitchell, "See 20 Years of Tuition Growth at National Universities," *U.S. News & World Report*, July 29, 2015.

14. "A Look at the Shocking Student Loan Debt Statistics for 2017," Student Loan Hero, accessed January 8, 2017. https://studentloanhero.com/student-loan-debt-statistics/

15. This and the following quotes are from Melanie Swan, interview with the authors, September 14, 2015.

16. Sony is working on this test-taking technology on the blockchain. See "Sony Global Education Develops Technology Using Blockchain," news release, February 22, 2016.

17. See Jane McGonigal, "How to Think (and Learn) Like a Futurist," SXSWedu keynote address, March 9, 2016.

18. See the Institute for the Future's *Learning Is Earning* 2026. https://www.iftf.org/learningisearning/

19. Vest, "Open Content and the Emerging Global Meta-University."

20. Katy Jordan, "MOOC Completion Rates: The Data," last updated June 12, 2015; "State of the MOOC 2016: A Year of Massive Landscape Change for Massive Open Online Courses," Online Course Report, accessed January 24, 2017. https://www.onlinecoursereport.com/state-of-the-mooc-2016-a-year-of-massive-landscape-change-for-massive-open-online-courses/

21. The term "global network for higher learning" was first developed by Don Tapscott and Anthony D. Williams in their book *Macrowikinomics: New Solutions for a Connected Planet* (New York: Portfolio Penguin, 2010). See also Don Tapscott and Anthony D. Williams, "Innovating the 21st-Century University: It's Time!" *EDUCAUSE Review* 45, no. 1 (January/February 2010).

22. Paul Hofheinz, "EU 2020: Why Skills Are Key for Europe's Future," *Lisbon Council Policy Brief* 4, no. 1 (2009).

# THE GLOBE AND MAIL

## Will Trump in Davos be the elephant in the china shop?

Don Tapscott, Toronto, ON, 22 January 2018. B4

DAVOS, SWITZERLAND—Last year I described him as "the elephant not in the room." This year he's more likely to be the elephant in the china shop.

The World Economic Forum starts in Davos on Monday—and there's a star attraction, or distraction, in US president Donald Trump. On the agenda of the Monday-to-Friday event: more than 400 sessions, with Mr. Trump scheduled to speak on Friday. On the minds of organizers: collaboration.

"We need collaborative efforts," forum founder and executive chairman Klaus Schwab said last week. "There is today a real danger of a collapse of our global systems. ... It is in our hands to change the state of the world."

For Mr. Trump, Davos sets up as an odd venue. The mission of the forum—this year's theme is Creating a Shared Future in a Fractured World—is to facilitate dialogue and rise above national interests to solve global problems. Mr. Trump's "America First" mantra is all about national interests.

Joining Mr. Trump will be hundreds of CEOs, 70 heads of state or government, 38 heads of major international organizations, and a record number of leaders from G7 economies. The opening address will be delivered by Narendra Modi, prime minister of India.

The forum is often accused of being a gabfest for the rich and powerful, and to be sure there will be plenty of that in Davos. But the organizers have made a concerted effort to be more inclusive. Nearly half of the proceedings, including Mr. Trump's speech, will be webcast. And there will be many representatives from international organizations, civil society, cultural and spiritual leaders, academia, labour, and the media. Also in attendance will be the largest-ever proportion of female leaders.

In addition, the meeting is the foremost global summit representing younger generations, with 50 members of the forum's Global Shaper community, aged between 20 and 30, and 80 Young Global Leaders under the age of 40, participating. Ultimately, these are the people responsible for shaping our rapidly evolving future.

There will also be thousands of entrepreneurs, academics, activists, and business people who, lacking a Davos invitation and the coveted white badge into the congress area, pour into town to hold events and meet in all the local hotels.

I have long believed that technologies such as the Internet would be the great leveller in our society. Like the World Economic Forum, it gave everyone a chance to contribute to the discussion. It provided a venue to tackle problems collectively.

But looking at the world in 2018, it seems I've so far been proved wrong. As Mr. Trump's presidency enters its second year, the discourse enabled by technological innovations is disjointed at best, and shattered at worst. Digital technologies themselves are at the heart of this fragmentation and polarization.

Around the world, especially in the United States, public faith in the electoral process is at an all-time low, undermined by hackers and claims of so-called fake news.

Mr. Trump won the 2016 election despite losing the popular vote. Then American intelligence agencies concluded the Russian government interfered with the electoral process using Internet-based tools.

It's just one example of the many challenges for our modern technology-driven society. How do we sort through all the misinformation spewed when a billion people essentially have printing presses at their fingertips?

How do we ensure the gathering of quality news in a world where the purpose of information is seemingly not to inform but to reinforce our own biases?

Two years ago, Mr. Schwab wrote a book called *The Fourth Industrial Revolution*. He believes we are in the early stages of a revolution that is fundamentally changing the way we live, work, and relate to one another. Ubiquitous, mobile supercomputing. Intelligent robots. Self-driving cars. Neuro-technological brain enhancements. Blockchain transactions bypassing intermediaries. Genetic editing. These changes are happening at exponential speed.

This month, Mr. Schwab released a follow-up book with forum executive Nicholas Davis: *Shaping the Fourth Industrial Revolution* argues we cannot let the many new technologies simply emerge. All of us need to help shape the future we want to live in. But what do we need to know and do to achieve this?

In my view, two new digital technologies—artificial intelligence and blockchain technology—are emerging as cornerstones to this revolution. But with revolution comes disruption, and evidence is mounting that we'll need a new social contract to deal with these massive innovations.

In the 20th century, countries built global institutions to facilitate joint action and address global problems. But let's face it—nation-states and their institutions, such as the G7 or the United Nations, are proving woefully inadequate in solving today's pernicious issues. The failure to come to agreements on everything from how to stop warlords or govern the global financial system is evidence that we need new tools and power structures.

The forum is probably the most important organization working on multi-stakeholder approaches to solving these problems. These issues will be at the forefront of the Davos discussion. I hope the Trump Show doesn't distract us too much—because, honestly, it's tough to imagine Mr. Trump having anything constructive to add to these debates. More likely he'll just be breaking a lot of china.

# MIT Press

## Toward a new social contract for the digital economy

Don Tapscott, Toronto, ON, January 2018

## Foreword to *Cyber Republic*

Writing the 20th-anniversary edition of my 1994 book, *The Digital Economy*, was a sobering experience. The book was very positive about the "promise of the Internet," and to be sure the Net has brought about many great innovations.

But the book has a small section about the Dark Side—things that could go wrong. Re-reading it 20 years later I was shocked to see that every danger I hypothesized has materialized.

One of my concerns was privacy. The digital economy has undermined our privacy through a system of "digital feudalism," wherein a tiny few have appropriated the largesse of this new era of prosperity. Data, the oil of the 21st century, is not owned by those who create it. Rather, it's controlled by an increasingly centralized group of "digital landlords," who collect, aggregate, and profit from the data that collectively constitutes our digital identities.

Exploiting our data has enabled them to achieve unprecedented wealth, while the middle class and prosperity have stalled.

In 1994 I'd hoped Internet would create new industries and jobs. It did for a while. But today technology is wiping out entire industries. Underemployment and the threat of structural employment are fuelling unrest. Trucking, one of Canada's largest sources of employment, will likely be automated within a decade. Digitized networks enable outsourcing, offshoring, and the globalization of labour. Within the second era of the digital age—one centred on blockchain technologies, machine learning, artificial intelligence, robotics, and the Internet of Things—many core functions of knowledge work, many companies and industries, are in jeopardy.

Yes, we've seen a new wave of entrepreneurism globally, but our regulations were designed for the old industrial economy and hamper success.

The increased transparency enabled by the Internet has also revealed deep problems in society. Canada is learning the truth about the horrific treatment of our Indigenous peoples who now have tools to speak out and organize collective action. We also understand deeply how climate change threatens civilization on this planet. People, especially young people who will suffer most, are now organizing to re-industrialize the country and the world.

I had hoped the Internet would bring us together as societies and improve our democracies. But the opposite has occurred. We often see only perspectives that reinforce our own views, with information filtered to accommodate our biases. The upshot has been more divisive public discourse, and democratic institutions are eroding before our eyes, as trust in politicians and the legitimacy of our governments is at an all-time low.

Populist rhetoric becomes more appealing in these conditions, and many are vulnerable to scapegoating and xenophobia. The upshot is there is a crisis of legitimacy of liberal democracy.

People everywhere are angry at career politicians who aren't seeing them, aren't listening to them, or aren't interested in their family's pain and suffering. Thus they have become vulnerable to populism, xenophobia, and scapegoating minority ethnic groups, races, and religions for the problems in their own lives.

Centrist parties are in rapid decline and extremist right-wing parties in Hungary, Poland, France, and Germany are on the rise. Perhaps as unthinkable as the success of Donald Trump is the rise of Bernie Sanders, an avowed socialist who came second to Joe Biden in the race for the Democratic Party's presidential candidate. The unfolding story is one of growing discontent with the deepening economic crisis and the old establishment that created it.

Conversely, the next era of the digital economy could bring epoch prosperity, with new networked models of global problem solving to realize such a dream. The reason is that we're entering a second era of the digital age. For the last 40 years we've seen the rise of mainframes, minicomputers, the PC, the Internet, mobility, the web, the mobile web, social media, the cloud, and big data.

We're entering a second era where new technologies are infusing into everything, and every business process. Innovations such as artificial intelligence (AI), machine learning, the Internet of Things (IoT), robotics, even technology in our bodies, drones, robots, and new materials are enabling entirely new types of enterprises. Foundational to these innovations is the underlying technology of crypto currencies—blockchain.

To meet these new challenges, the time has come for every country to reimagine its social contract—the basic expectation between business, government, and civil society.

When countries evolved from an agrarian economy to an industrial one, we developed a new social contract for the times—public education; a social safety net; securities legislation; laws about pollution, crime, traffic, workplace safety; countless nongovernmental civil society organizations arose to help solve problems.

It is time to update these agreements, create new institutions, and renew the expectations and responsibilities that citizens should have about society. I've spent considerable time working on a framework for such a new social contract and have come to some pretty far-reaching conclusions.

We need new models of identity, moving away from the industrial-age system of stamps, seals, and signatures we depend on to this day. We need to protect the security of personhood and end the system of digital feudalism. Individuals should own and profit from the data they create. We need new laws for the development and usage of autonomous vehicles, robots, drones, and technology in our bodies as well as the data these innovations throw off.

Our basic expectations of work are shifting, but our systems designed to support workers have not. Gone are the days when a worker might expect to do the same job or work in the same field their whole career. Students today are preparing for unprecedented lifelong learning, with the knowledge that technology will likely force them to reimagine their role in the workforce.

In the face of new models of work, we need to update our educational institutions to prepare for this kind of lifelong learning and establish a universal basic income to support transition periods, providing a foundation for entrepreneurialism and investing in the potential of our populations.

We must adopt new models for citizen engagement in our government. In AI and blockchain we have found one such model, with the possibility of embedding electoral promises into smart contracts. Meanwhile, it enables secure outlets for online voting and other forms of direct democracy using the platforms voters use every day.

Networks enable citizens to participate fully in their own governance, and we can now move to a second era of democracy based on a culture of public deliberation and active citizenship. Mandatory voting encourages active, engaged, and responsible citizens.

We also need business leaders to participate responsibly—for their own long-term survival and the health of the economy overall. Even—or especially—in a time of exploding information online, we need scientists, researchers, and a professional Fourth Estate of journalists to seek the truth, examine options, and inform the ongoing public discourse. We each have new responsibilities to inform ourselves in a world where the old ways are failing.

Are these expectations overly ambitious or even utopian? I think not. Nothing is more powerful than an idea that's time has come, and the challenges facing our economic and political institutions today warrant such a change.

The challenges of our era demand audacious solutions. Now more than ever the world needs fresh thinking for a new digital age.

Which is why I am delighted to write this foreword to *Cyber Republic*—an extraordinary book by George Zarkadakis. Democracy is in deep trouble. Legitimacy is the idea that you may disagree with who is in power, but you think the system is a good one. But more and more people are challenging democracy itself, including Donald

Trump, who said voting is rigged and the centre of democracy in the United States is a "swamp." Youth voting in many countries is at an all-time low and according the 2020 Edelman Trust Barometer, trust in governments has never been lower in modern history.

It's time for change and George makes the case effectively with deep research, strong argumentation, and vivid examples. He calls for a rethinking of our systems of democracy and of the social contract itself. Like me, you may not agree with everything in the book, but you will find it enormously stimulating and helpful.

There is a "demand pull" to reinvent democracy, given the current crisis and the new requirements for government. As George eloquently points out, there is also a "technology push" coming from the second era of the digital age—the age of intelligent machines.

It is my hope that many will read the book and that it will help us catalyse a global discussion. Read on, debate, and let's take action!

# QUARTZ

## Taking back our identities, our data, and our autonomy in the digital economy

DON TAPSCOTT, 11 SEPTEMBER 2019

## Serfing the Internet

### The end of digital feudalism

We're over two decades into an era of digital feudalism.

Feudalism is a centuries-old concept. In medieval times, the nobility owned vast amounts of land. Serfs worked the land to create value, but most of that value was confiscated by the landlord.

Instead of farm produce, today the new asset class is data—created by us, but captured by digital landlords such as social media companies, search engines, online retailers, governments, and banks. "Surfing the Internet" has become "serfing the Internet," with users giving up intimate details of their lives for the Internet lordships to aggregate, expropriate, and monetize. We, as the serfs, only get left with a few lousy cabbages.

This is important, because this data isn't just the by-product of your labour. It is the stuff of your identity in the digital age.

All this data constitutes a "virtual you." The digital crumbs that you leave in daily life create a mirror image that knows more about you than you do. You probably can't remember dozens of your personal identifiers: your driver's licence details, credit card numbers, government information. But you definitely don't know your exact location a year ago; what you bought or what amount of money you transacted; what you said online; or what medication you took or diagnosis you received.

And that's just the beginning. In the future, the virtual you will contain detailed medical information like your heart rate, blood pressure, or myriad other real-time measures of what you do, how you function, where you are, and even how you feel.

The trouble is that the virtual you is not owned by you. "Imagine if General Motors did not pay for its steel, rubber, or glass—its inputs," economist Robert J. Shapiro once said. "That's what it's like for the big Internet companies. It's a sweet deal."

We create the asset; they expropriate it. Yet we still thank them for use of their land, rather than demanding what is rightfully ours.

## Why should you care?

There are problems with this new form of feudalism:

- First, we can't use our own data to plan our lives. It's stored in other people's silos, which we can't access—but third parties like Cambridge Analytica can, often without our knowledge.

- Second, we enjoy none of the rewards of this third-party data usage, yet we bear most of the risk and responsibility for its clean-up, should they lose or abuse our data.

- Third, these elites are invading our privacy and telling us to "get over it," when they know full well that privacy is the foundation of freedom; just look at the Chinese social credit scoring system.

- Fourth, we can't monetize these data assets for ourselves, resulting in a bifurcation of wealth and all its discontents.

The serfs are getting mad as hell and aren't going to take it anymore. But populism, from Brexit to Trump, is not the solution. Nor is the European Union's General Data Protection Regulation (GDPR), which is a partial measure at best, and hypocritical in light of the new EU common identity repository. Nor is a heads-will-roll type of policy that calls for the breakup of Amazon, Facebook, and Google for violating anti-monopoly laws.

What we need is a wholesale shift in how we define and assign ownership of data assets and how we establish, manage, and protect our identities in a digital world. Change *those* rules, and we end up changing *everything*. It is a revolution to be sure.

We've called it the blockchain revolution.

## The self-sovereign identity

State-run Internet-based systems are problematic. In the last ten years, at least 48 government databases have been breached, exposing the data of 1.44 billion people—and that number doesn't include hacks to government-managed health care and education records. Yet we're dependent on system administrators who can freeze access, delete our voter registration or other credentials, and use banks, telecoms, and tech firms to surveil us.

Nothing about these institution-centric systems is citizen-friendly. They discriminate against the poor, the rural, the homeless, the imprisoned, and the overworked in society. Syrian refugees in particular put a spotlight on the crisis of state-based identification.

The reality of a government-sourced and -sanctioned identity is untenable—both administratively and philosophically. Why should any government get to rubber-stamp who we are? We should be establishing our own identities and, as Joseph Lubin of ConsenSys wrote, bootstrapping ourselves into economic enfranchisement. We need to take action now.

What each of us needs is a self-sovereign and inalienable digital identity, one that is neither bestowed nor revocable by any central administrator and is enforceable in any context, in person and online, anywhere in the world.

As Alex Tapscott and I argue in *Blockchain Revolution*, the means now exist to assert what developer Devon Leffreto calls "sovereign source authority": identity is not simply endowed at birth; it is endowed *by* birth.

# Here's how it works

## A list of identity commons

To bootstrap our identity, we first need a model that is distributed among and maintained by the people whose identities it protects. This means that everyone's incentives align in an identity commons, with clear rights for users to steward their own identity, protect their privacy, access (and allow others to access) and monetize their own data, and participate in rule-making around the preservation and usage of the commons.

Each identity is in a black box on a blockchain. It sweeps up the exhaust of all our daily transactional and information data—from purchases to our biological data—protecting it and enabling each of us to use it any way we want.

Several identity projects in the blockchain space are working to provide such structure and capabilities.

- *Blockstack,* a public-benefit corporation in Delaware, incorporates the Bitcoin blockchain in its open-source identity solution. Blockstack users can set the location of their user profile and application data, and Blockstack has no control over the identity information on the Bitcoin blockchain or stored on Blockstack's peer-to-peer network.

- *Civic,* a for-profit company based in San Francisco, offers an ID verification solution through an Ethereum-based platform. Users collect verifiable claims of attributes from validators—such as banks, governments, and universities—but when a third party wants to learn something about a user, the user can decide whether and how much to reveal. The third party must then pay the validator of the relevant attribute, which is an incentive for validators to participate.

- *Sovrin* is an identity platform governed by the nonprofit Sovrin Foundation and running on a distributed ledger based on Hyperledger Indy. The nodes maintaining the ledger are trusted entities such as banks, colleges, governments, and nongovernmental organizations, which are approved by the Sovrin Foundation Board of Trustees. Users download the Connect.Me wallet app for storing their credentials and cryptographic tokens, as well as communicating with other wallets for peer-to-peer exchanges of data, which are stored locally in the user's wallet or encrypted cloud backup.

- *uPort,* a platform built on the Ethereum network and funded by for-profit ConsenSys in New York, enables users to create a decentralized identity (DID) based on the proposed ERC-1056 lightweight Ethereum identity standard for Ethereum wallets. The app manages user identities and credentials, such as keys, identities, and attestations, which are portable across service providers and client applications. The app can authenticate a user and disclose verifiable claims to whomever the user chooses.

- *Veres One,* a blockchain operating under the guidance of the Veres One W3C Community Group, may be the simplest self-sovereign identity infrastructure. It has no tokens and stores no user data—it stores only the DIDs used for key management and service endpoints discovery. Through Veres One, anyone with a web browser can generate a DID compatible with other identity services, allowing for portability.

Many of these startups are collaborating in the Decentralized Identity Foundation, a consortium consisting of Hyperledger and

R3, and incumbents such as Accenture, Microsoft, and IBM. Its working groups are focusing on three big areas—identifiers and discovery, storage and computation of data, and attestation and reputation—with an eye to developing use-cases and standards.

## Breaking free of our digital landlords

The ultimate solution, however, must exist independent of any corporation, government, or other third party and should not be subject to the agency risk of executives or political parties. It must interoperate with these institutions, even as it outlasts them. In fact, it must be built to *outlive* its users and enforce their right to be forgotten. This would mean separating data rights from the actual data, so that the rights holder could delete it. To be inclusive, it must be user-friendly with a low-tech mobile interface and low-cost dispute resolution.

This transition will take time. We expect organizations to take at least three actions to rebuild the trust of those whose data they hold.

The first involves governance. Many large corporations and government agencies have strong governance mechanisms for their hard assets, but really poor governance of information assets. Companies must define decision rights around their data and develop an accountability framework that disciplines how employees use data.

The second involves the discontinuation of practices that collect and store customer data. This could involve either destroying these massive customer databases altogether (after returning files and records to customers) or migrating this data to distributed storage systems, such as the IPFS, and then transferring control to customers.

The third involves the cultivation of a new core competence: the ability to work with huge anonymized datasets rented from large numbers of people, all handled in a distributed and trust-minimized manner. It will remove data as a toxic asset from the corporate balance sheet and make it a fundamental human asset from birth. It will flip the data-analytics business model on its head and reward corporations for serving as data brokers on behalf of individuals. This will see the end of the large centralized data frackers that scrape, hoard, and rent, but don't protect this data.

These new approaches to privacy and ID management give citizens ownership of their identities, the facts of their existence, and the data they create as they live their lives. The self-sovereign identity is one of the pillars of a new social contract for the digital economy and will be critical to the transformation to a more open, inclusive, and private economy.

We need more than access to some of our data. We should own it.

# The Globe and Mail

## Trent University's founding president Thomas Henry Bull Symons was "a beacon of intellectual light"

### Don Tapscott, Toronto, ON, 5 January 2021

*As a first-year student at Trent University, I had the pleasure of meeting the university's founding president, Thomas Henry Bull Symons. Over the next decades, he profoundly influenced my life and the lives of so many others. In 2013, I became chancellor of the university, retiring last year, and in that capacity worked with him again. He passed away January 1, 2020. I was deeply honoured to write his obituary. This obituary was published today in Canada's national newspaper,* The Globe and Mail.

Thomas Henry Bull Symons was internationally renowned as a distinguished professor and author in Canadian Studies and academic administrator. One of his crowning achievements was helping found Trent University in Peterborough, Ontario. It opened its doors to its first 102 students in the 1964–65 academic year. Professor Symons served for 11 years as Trent's first president and vice-chancellor. His biographer describes Professor Symons as "one of Canada's pre-eminent educational and cultural statesmen of the 20th century."

"Tom was a builder," said Canadian ambassador to the United Nations Bob Rae of Professor Symons, who died at home on January 1 at the age of 91. "He was a unique figure in our country because he had a vital interest and impact on so many areas—higher education, heritage, the environment, Indigenous Studies, and understanding Canada. To me he was the progenitor of Canadian Studies. He just built things."

Former prime minister Paul Martin was a second-year history student at the University of Toronto when he first met Professor Symons. "He led a small discussion group, which everybody wanted to belong to because quite simply he made history live," Mr. Martin said. "In the years that followed we became good friends and when I began to pursue my interest in Indigenous matters, Tom's work at Trent University stood out for me as an example of what should be done. We will all miss him."

In May 2019, Ontario lieutenant-governor Elizabeth Dowdeswell joined dignitaries from the Peterborough area and more than 400 students, alumni, friends, family, and community leaders to celebrate Professor Symons's 90th birthday.

Ms. Dowdeswell befriended Professor Symons decades ago and would often visit with him and his wife at Marchbanks, their home in Peterborough. "Every time I drove to Ottawa I would try to stop on the way to have a cup of tea with him and Christine," she said. "I walked into that lovely house, just full of books, fire burning, and we would have a rich conversation. He was a beacon of intellectual light and Canadian scholarship. You'd always leave feeling enriched by the experience."

After hearing of his death, Ms. Dowdeswell tweeted, "He loved this country and brought this love to the world. His legacy is an inspiration and his contributions will continue to benefit all those who seek understanding and who ask the great Canadian questions."

Former students describe how Professor Symons would introduce himself to them on campus, knowing their names without ever having met them. Apparently, each year he memorized names, photographs, and some pertinent information about members of the incoming class. Such behaviour fit his highly personalized model of pedagogy and student culture at Trent—the little "Oxford on the Otonabee" as it was called in the early days.

Said current Trent president Leo Groarke, "I believe he knew he could foster that culture through his own example and words, showing that he cared and was prepared to do the background research and study."

Speaking at the 90th birthday celebration, former student Stu Butts used a metaphor of a honeybee to describe Professor Symons's impact on postsecondary education in Canada and beyond.

"As a scholar, educator, instigator, collaborator, pollinator, and friend, Tom has brought life and sustenance to an untold number of associations, organizations, institutions, and endeavours. We are proud of the fact that we have been able to keep our 'bee' at Trent, in Peterborough, while at the same time sharing him with the world."

Trent University was created after a committee of Peterborough citizens approached Professor Symons in 1961 while he was a dean at the University of Toronto. The citizens wanted Professor Symons to lead a campaign to create a university in their city. Professor Symons embraced the opportunity.

"The organization of the university and its general character is a pretty pronounced departure from the current trend in higher education in Canada and still more in the United States," Professor Symons told CBC Radio in 1969. "At a time when higher education is moving toward mass production, huge institutions, huge classes, and depersonalization of the whole process of higher education, this university is moving in the other direction. [We want] as small classes as we can possibly manage, toward as much opportunity as possible for faculty and students to know one another and work together, and toward the best possible opportunities for the individual student to develop in an individual way."

Professor Symons feared institutions of higher education, including his beloved University of Toronto, were becoming akin to "impersonal factories" where an "academic elephantiasis" of unchecked growth diminished the educational experience.

With Professor Symons as president, Trent University created Canada's first Indigenous Studies program, followed by the Canadian Studies program and the *Journal of Canadian Studies*. Interdisciplinary learning in the liberal arts and sciences is a defining quality of Trent. Professor Symons said it was England's Durham University that helped inspire Trent's federation of small, interdisciplinary colleges.

Professor Symons viewed Trent as his baby and remained active in campus life until his death. Several of Trent's subsequent presidents report that he continued to express his views forcefully to them on various matters such as campus architecture, his beloved college system, and the university's strategy, whether these views were solicited or not.

After graduating from the University of Toronto (BA 1951), Professor Symons attended Oriel College, at Oxford (BA 1953, M.A. 1957). Professor Symons returned to the University of Toronto, where he was a tutor in history at Trinity College, 1953–55, and then dean of Devonshire House, University of Toronto, 1955–63.

Professor Symons was Trent's president and vice-chancellor until 1972, and in 1979, he was named the Vanier Professor. Upon retirement in 1994, he was made Vanier Professor Emeritus, and a Trent campus was renamed after him.

In the early 1970s, Professor Symons led a national commission on Canadian Studies. The commission's report, titled "To Know Ourselves," was widely praised and inspired many scholars.

In 1976, he became a member of the Order of Canada (later promoted to companion, the order's highest level), and he was elected as a fellow of the Royal Society of Canada in 1977.

Professor Symons was awarded the Order of Ontario in 2002, in part recognizing his contribution to the province by mediating high-profile French-language disputes in Sturgeon Falls in 1971 and in Cornwall in 1973. From the funds he received for this work, he set up the annual Symons Award for Excellence in Teaching, which continues to honour the best instructors at Trent University.

As Ontario's Commissioner of Human Rights from 1975 to 1978, he helped lead major advancements, particularly for the LGBT community.

Professor Symons served on the boards of various corporations, including being chair of the Social Responsibility Committee at Celanese Canada Inc. Professor Symons also had a long working relationship with Czech-born shoe company owner Thomas J. Bata, with whom he worked closely during Trent University's early years.

Internationally, Professor Symons was chairman of the Association of Commonwealth Universities and chair of the International Board and vice-president of the International Council of United World Colleges. In 1982, Professor Symons was the first Canadian to receive the Distinguished Service to Education Award of the globe-spanning Council for the Advancement and Support of Education.

Professor Symons received 13 honorary degrees from Canadian universities and colleges, and he played a role in the founding of more than a dozen other colleges and universities. His work in the creation of Peterborough's Sacred Heart College resulted in a knighthood from the Vatican.

One incident illustrated the deep affection Professor Symons inspired everywhere he went. The late 1960s were a time of campus protest across North America. Trent had its first demonstration in March 1968, and Professor Symons, then the university's president, was the target.

But there was a twist. A group of students learned that Professor Symons had been approached by the Conservative Party in Ottawa to take on a new major political role in Canada. More than 375 of Trent's 750 students demonstrated outside the president's office, encouraging him to stay at Trent. Signs read "Keep the President Resident" and "Oh no please don't go." One of the student organizers, Stephen Stohn (now Trent's chancellor), said: "We wanted him to know how much we appreciated his vision for the university and admired him personally."

Professor Symons declined the Ottawa opportunity and served as Trent president for another five years, although he did become chair of a new Conservative Party initiative, the National Policy Advisory Committee.

Thomas Henry Bull Symons was born in Toronto on May 30, 1929, son of First World War flying ace Harry Lutz Symons and the former Dorothy Bull, daughter of the financier and historian William Perkins Bull. He married Christine Ryerson on August 17, 1963, and leaves her, as well as his children, Mary, Ryerson, and Jeffrey; and grandchildren, Wilson, Leighton, Ava, Charlotte, and Olivia.

# CREDITS

*The author and publisher gratefully acknowledge the following publications who granted permission to reprint articles in this book. Any articles not cited here appear courtesy Don Tapscott. Photo credits appear with each respective photo.*

"A Bretton Woods for the 21st Century" on pages 103 to 105 was originally published in *Harvard Business Review*, March 2014. Copyright 2014 by Harvard Business Publishing; all rights reserved. Reprinted with permission.

"After 20 Years, It's Harder to Ignore the Digital Economy's Dark Side" on pages 121 to 127 was originally published March 2016 in hbr.org. Copyright 2016 by Harvard Business Publishing; all rights reserved. Reprinted with permission.

"One of the world's most influential management thinkers on how the modern firm is changing" on pages 154 to 158 was originally published May 17, 2016, in *The Australian*. The use of this work has been licensed by Copyright Agency except as permitted by the Copyright Act, you must not re-use this work without the permission of the copyright owner or Copyright Agency."

"How Blockchain Is Changing Finance" by Alex Tapscott and Don Tapscott on pages 159 to 164 was originally published March 2017 in hbr.org. Copyright 2017 by Harvard Business Publishing; all rights reserved. Reprinted with permission.

"The Blockchain Revolution and Higher Education" on pages 165 to 187 was originally published as Don Tapscott and Alex Tapscott, "The Blockchain Revolution and Higher Education," *EDUCAUSE Review* 52, no. 2 (March/April 2017). Reprinted with permission.

# NAME AND PLACE INDEX

# ABOUT THE AUTHOR

**Don Tapscott** is one of the world's leading authorities on the impact of technology on business and society. He has authored 16 widely read books about the digital age including *Paradigm Shift* (1993), *The Digital Economy* (1995), *Growing Up Digital* (1998), *Digital Capital* (2000), *The Naked Corporation* (2002), and *Wikinomics: How Mass Collaboration Changes Everything*—the #1 best-selling management book of 2007—which has been translated into over 25 languages.

In 2016, during his first term as chancellor of Trent University, Don co-authored *Blockchain Revolution: How the Technology Behind Bitcoin and Other Cryptocurrencies Is Changing the World* with his son, Alex Tapscott. According to the late Harvard Professor Clay Christensen, it is "the book, literally, on how to survive and thrive in this next wave of technology-driven disruption."

In 2017, Don and Alex co-founded the Blockchain Research Institute, which is conducting the definitive investigation into the enterprise applications of distributed ledger technologies and the "trivergence" of blockchain, artificial intelligence, and the Internet of Things.

Don is a member of the Order of Canada, and an adjunct professor at INSEAD. He was ranked the second most influential Management Thinker in the world and the top Digital Thinker by Thinkers50 before his induction into the Thinkers50 Hall of Fame. He lives in Toronto with his wife, Ana P. Lopes, C.M.